SNOWBIRDS UNLIMITED

Tales from the Restless Traveler

Marilyn Catherine McDonald, MA

SNOWBIRDS UNLIMITED

What people say about Snowbirds Unlimited – the book:

"I had the pleasure of editing Marilyn McDonald's travel stories for RV Life, and she was a delight to work with. She always brought a fresh perspective to the places she visited and wrote vivid and succinct accounts of her experiences. I'm sure that many of our readers were inspired to take similar trips after reading her stories on Chaco Canyon in New Mexico, the Steens Mountain in Oregon, the Gold Rush trail in California, and other places that she brought to life so well."

– Mike Ward, editor, RV Life Magazine

"Just glancing through your writing credits it appears you have more than enough interesting material for the snowbirds book. Count me in as an interested reader and purchaser when the time comes."

– Brooke Snavely, editor, Sunriver Scene

Other books by Marilyn Catherine McDonald, MA

Little Girl Lost
A True Story of a Tragic Death

Mother of Eight Survives Population Explosion
"Just Between Us" Column Selections

Alert the Media
How the American Indian Movement used the Mass Media
Adapted from 1977 University of Portland Masters Thesis
"The Interrelationship between the
American Indian Movement (AIM) and the Mass Media"

Columns under the title, Snowbirds Unlimited: Tales from the Restless Traveler may have first appeared in the La Pine Newberry Eagle, 9/04-9/09. Although updated or revised they remain the sole property of this author.

Certain articles used in this book, although updated or revised, may have first appeared in one or more of the following: Western RV News & Recreation, RV Life Magazine, Transitions Abroad Magazine, Highways Magazine, The American Legion Magazine, and other print or electronic media. All published articles granted "first NA rights only" and remain the sole property of this author.

So, little snowbird,
take me with you when you go
to that land of gentle breezes
where the peaceful waters flow…

"Snowbird" – a song made popular by
Canadian Singer Anne Murray

PREFACE

Snow falls each year before we leave Central Oregon for the winter.

It is a light dusting that doesn't last. It is a lovely reminder of what we once enjoyed. I put my cross-country skis in a garage sale before I moved to La Pine in 1999, knowing we would be spending our winters in Mexico.

I still have enough kid in me to appreciate the falling snowflakes. So, I take my camera with me for a walk in the woods, signaling the end of summer – marking our migration south.

When I started searching for answers to why we are called snowbirds, I ran across the lyrics of Anne Murray's song, as well as an encyclopedia section on the Junco, or snowbird, relative of the finches. Slate-colored Juncos breed in northern evergreen forests of Canada and the United States, and are found as far south as the Gulf of Mexico.

Canadians and Americans have been heading south for decades, if not centuries, to escape the cold sting of winter. You need only drive on Oregon Highway 97 from late September through December to see the migration of recreational vehicles (RVs) heading to warmer climates, and as early as March on their return. These "houses on the road" have grown in size and luxury so that many of the "snowbirds" are full timers.

For seven years, we traveled south in a 20-foot self-contained RV. We started leaving the RV at home and traveling by car when the price of gas escalated. Fortunately, we have a small house and everything we need in Mexico.

In Australia the retired travelers are called "grey nomads." Grey nomads primarily are people who have sold their homes and travel on a continuous basis. Perhaps that better describes what many of our friends and neighbors in Mexico do throughout the year. We still have roots, with houses in La Pine, Oregon and San Felipe, Mexico. Without roots I might consider myself "homeless."

Many Canadian as well as American snowbirds live in our San Felipe neighborhood. We even have friends from Switzerland and Germany there in the winter. When anyone asks our neighbor,

"What do you do in Mexico?" Bill responds, "I don't know, but it takes us all day to do it."

So, along with the Junco seeking warmth, we sing "Spread your tiny wings and fly away." See you again in the spring.

DEDICATION

This book is dedicated to my husband Harry Taylor,
devoted traveling companion, the love of my life.

ACKNOWLEDGEMENTS

First and foremost, I must acknowledge my parents, Mary and Angus McDonald. They woke me and my brother up in the middle of the night "to get an early start" on our vacations to my grandparents in Pennsylvania or Maine. Still drowsy, in our pajamas, with pillows and blankets, we were tucked in the backseat of the car and continued our sleep. My mother woke me from time to time saying, "Wake up, you're missing all the beautiful scenery." I learned to love travel.

Thanks, as well, to my husband Harry Taylor, my wonderful traveling companion since 1998. We have, indeed, seen a whole lot of this shrinking planet. I want to express my appreciation for his 26 years of military service to our country. His service has provided us with many benefits. And, for his patience while I spend hours at the computer, researching and writing. Most of all, thanks for the encouragement.

I extend my appreciation to a young man named Justin Snyder, editor of his family's publication Western RV News and Recreation when we launched the travel writing segment of my career. Many thanks as well to Mike Ward, editor of RV Life Magazine, for the many opportunities to turn my travels into articles. Additional thanks go to editors of a variety of newspapers and magazines for carrying my stories.

Editors of the Newberry Eagle, during my stint from 9/04 to 9/09, are remembered and appreciated for hard work under difficult financial times for the publication. They kept the Newberry Eagle going. The publication was started and partially funded by the La Pine Community Action Team, filling a gap in the local communication network. As a member of their advisory panel and contributor, my writing wants meshed with their publication needs. We did some really good things.

Some good things ended for me in 2009 when I stopped the travel writing and left space in my life for new challenges. This book is a natural outgrowth of those many years of travel writing. The time of writing specifically for travel publications may have ended, but our travels continue.

Recently, I spoke with a group of senior citizens about journaling and preserving their life stories. When I finished, a woman tapped me on the shoulder and asked, "Do you have the Lord in your life?" I simply responded, "Yes, I do." So, I must acknowledge "the God of my understanding," without Whom, I can do nothing.

CONTENTS

INTRODUCTION

GETTING FROM HERE TO THERE

L ife is a journey, not a destination. For all the travels we do, it is quite evident that the majority of our time is spent getting from one place to another.

In my youth I traveled extensively with my parents. During my 25-year first marriage, and with my eight children, I traveled extensively. My 22 years between marriages, when I was a working single parent, I traveled extensively. Now, Harry and I, our life together is about getting from here to there – by car, by RV by train, by plane, by ship. Oh yes, we travel the globe. We log mucho miles.

I can't imagine a life without travel. In my first marriage I moved from Ferndale, Michigan to Roswell, New Mexico, and back. Then moved from Michigan to California, where we moved three times. We then moved from California to Beaverton, Oregon, where I lived in the same house for over 30 years. I sold the house when children were all grown and gone, and moved into a penthouse apartment for 18 months. Later, I moved back to a condo in Beaverton.

Harry's son Dee and my daughter Sheila had been together for 20 years when Harry's wife Geri passed. That branch of my family tree was living in Anchorage, Alaska at the time. Through chance encounters while visiting our family, Harry and I became better friends.

In April of 1998, I had a three-week vacation planned for Italy and Amsterdam. I spent eleven days in Rome during Easter week. Harry thought he might like to join me in Italy. He flew into Rome at the end of my time there. We had a car rental and began our first journey together to parts of Italy and then to Amsterdam. First we went north to Siena and Florence, then south to Sorrento, the Amalfi Coast, the Isle of Capri, and Pompeii. I depended on *Rick Steves' Italy 1997* book to get us from here to there.

Arriving in Amsterdam on separate flights, we boarded the train to a city center hotel. While in Amsterdam we enjoyed an evening boat ride through the canals. We took a bus tour to the windmills and dikes, and took a train to see acres of tulips. It was all magical and wonderful. Travel is what we love to do.

The November following the trip to Italy, I quit my day job and we traveled four months throughout the Southwestern United States in Harry's Roadtrek 190 RV.

We had no intention of traveling into Mexico during our pre-nuptial tour of the southwest. However, when we were in the Yuma, Arizona, visitors center I spotted a flyer that offered a guided caravan tour to El Dorado Ranch, in San Felipe, Baja Norte, Mexico. For $99, we traveled down the Baja with a 36 other vehicles and spent seven days at the El Dorado Ranch RV Park overlooking the Sea of Cortez.

Following a second week parked on the beach in downtown San Felipe, we went back to the ranch and bought a lot, our first purchase of property together. Watching the lights on the shrimp boats at night, and the spectacular sunrises coming out of the Sea of Cortez, I was hooked.

We traveled from Mexico back into Arizona, and during our week in Sedona, Harry proposed. By the time we reached Oregon we had a draft for a small house ready to fax to the architect at the ranch in Mexico. You may want to look for this story about "Building in Baja, and Other Lifestyle Changes" that appears much later in this book.

We married August 14, 1999, at an historical farmhouse in Beaverton, with most of our integrated family present. His son and my daughter were our attendants, and then helped us move me to La Pine, in Central Oregon.

We moved into our casita in February 2000, and took an extensive road trip out of there about two months later. In an effort to reach Naples, Florida, before my daughter Sheila, Harry's son Dee, and our grandchildren returned to Alaska from visiting my daughter Mary and her family, we traveled 300 to 400 miles each day. Some of that trip through southern states is a blur. I want to see New Orleans again, now recovered after Katrina nearly buried the city.

After visiting family in Florida, we headed up the Atlantic Coastline, hitting all the major points of interest. Part of that story, in reference to Washington, DC, is in "Life's History Lessons" later in this book.

That first year leaving Mexico, we came back to La Pine by way of Florida, South and North Carolina, Washington, DC, Kansas City, Salt Lake City, and parts of Idaho. On another adventure we came back through Lake Powell and Bryce Canyon. We have journeyed back to La Pine, Oregon, by way of California Highway 1 and the Mission Trail; Yosemite and the California Highway 49 Gold Rush Trail. We stopped in Flagstaff, Arizona and Santa Fe, New Mexico, as well as Chaco and other canyons. We even came back to La Pine by way of Egypt. But, that's another story.

We visit friends on the way to and from Mexico. We make one Oregon Coast trip each summer and incorporate visits to family and friends. Without our calendar, we wouldn't know where we were supposed to be. I have a "Getting Ready to Go" list for La Pine and one for San Felipe.

We thank God each time we have once again safely completed the journey from there to here. And trust we will have more journeys from here to there – wherever "there" is.

*The best cure for restlessness for far away places is to go there
and find them full of people who would like to get back home again.*

Madam Swetchine, a Russian mystic (1782-1857)

1

THIS LAND IS OUR LAND

Woody Guthrie said it in his song *This Land Is Your Land* which has become a national folk anthem. In 1945, Smokey Bear started saying "Only you can prevent forest fires." Woodsy Owl began telling it like it is on America's first Earth Day in 1970, when he said, "Give a Hoot – Don't Pollute." A later message from Woodsy told his friends "Lend a Hand – Care for the Land."

For those Americans who say, "My land, love it or leave it," the United States Department of Agriculture Forest Service (USDAFS), the designated custodian of nearly 200 million acres of public land, might want to respond with, "Leave it like you found it – or better."

Actually, the USDAFS has the welcome mat out for all visitors to "our land." On the USDA Forest Service web site *Special Places Newsletter: A Travel and Tourism Planner's Guide to Your National Forests*, September 2001, the Message from the Chief Dale N. Bosworth stated:

"America's national forests and grasslands are the 'golden crown' of outdoor settings where national and international visitors alike can enjoy a wide variety of premier adventure travel and ecotourism recreation activities. From Alaska's forests and glaciers, Idaho's wild rivers, Utah's and Colorado's ski mountains,

New Mexico's Jemez Mountains heritage, to Caribbean tropical forests, I invite you to visit your national forests for outdoor fun and experiences of a lifetime."

From its home page, you can go to a variety National Forest web site, their National Headquarters, Fire Information, or Work with the Forest Service links. The Reservations link (www.reserveusa. com) will be particularly helpful to RV, trailer, fifth wheel and camper visitors who prefer to know where they are going and what is required. For instance, if you enjoy fishing remote lakes, rivers and streams you can reserve a "unique cabin in either the Chugah or Tongass National Forests, located in majestic and scenic Alaska."

Other options include reserving one or more of over 49,000 campsites provided by the Corps of Engineers and the Forest Service. When you're looking for pristine wilderness experience, contact Boundary Waters Canoe Area Wilderness (BWCAW) for your wilderness permit reservations. And, when the summer heats up with wildfires you can get information about high-risk areas, restrictions and conditions.

Summertime, and the living is easier for travelers to any one of the nations 155 national forests or 21 national grasslands when they know and respect the advice of the USDA Forest Service. It does not go unnoticed when the USDAFS butts heads with hunters, fishers, ranchers and farmers over land and water usage. However, as responsible guardians of the land ourselves, we can only respect and follow Forest Service guidelines.

The USDA Forest Service has invited the travel and tourism industry to join them in "promoting the development of responsible, sustainable recreation on the land. As visitors leave the beaten track and venture off from our developed facilities, we have adopted a major tool for educating tourists and recreational users on ways to conserve our public lands. This tool is Leave No Trace, Inc."

Leave No Trace (LNT) is a nonprofit education program uniting the Forest Service, National Park Service, Bureau of Land Management, and US Fish and Wildlife Service – with manufacturers, outdoor retailers, user groups, educators, and individuals who share their commitment to public lands.

"The mission of Leave No Trace is to promote and inspire responsible outdoor recreation through education, research, and partnerships." It is about the future for communities of peoples, plants, and animals.

Fire is the greatest, but not the only, threat to our national forest lands. The Forest Service estimates "fires burn about 12 million acres of forest land annually – destroying timber crops and damaging watershed lands, kill or maim large numbers of animals, and destroy recreational and scenic values of the land."

According to the Forest Service, people cause most wildfires. However, lightening strikes that ignite dry underbrush start many fires as well.

In the summer, we live deep in the woods along the Deschutes River, 11 miles from La Pine in Central Oregon. A few years ago, an unattended campfire ignited a wildfire that burned nine acres and took three days to fully contain, three miles from our house. A month later, a campfire left for dead, smoldered and started a two-acre blaze less than two miles from our house.

The following summer, a US Forest Service information team paid us a visit. The Crane Complex Fires, eight miles west of us, were ignited by lightening and eventually burned 720 acres of forest. The combined fires were 40 percent contained. The Forest Service people pointed out the fire and our location on the map, and went over our evacuation plan and exit route. They left a 12-page copy of "Living with Fire: a guide for the homeowner." The final, bold-print statement was "Most importantly, STAY CALM!" Easy for them to say! We were making our list of what to have ready to take with us.

Approximately 400 personnel from as far away as Colorado, Indiana and North Carolina and three water-spraying helicopters contained the fire the following day. Eight or more national, state and local agencies were involved in that fire alone.

It takes hundreds and thousands of personnel to put out wildfires throughout the country during each high-risk, dry season. In addition, it takes thousands of paid personnel and volunteers to provide the services that maintain our national parks and forest lands.

In 2002, the Forest Service sought volunteers to conduct field interviews of visitors to a select number of recreational use sites over a two-year period. Interviewers were asked for a one-month commitment, and "secret shoppers" who will drive or walk through certain interview points were asked for as little as a few hours. They were interviewed and reported back to the coordinator.

Volunteer opportunities as well as seasonal/temporary, paid positions are available with the US Forest Service, State Parks, or the National Parks System, which is a bureau of the Department of the Interior. See the FS Retiree web page or call 707-574-6233 for information.

Yosemite became second U.S. National Park, 1890

In 1872, Yellowstone became the first of more than 300 national park units covering 76 million acres. The National Park Service was created in 1916 to "conserve scenery and the natural and historic objects and wildlife therein, and to provide for the enjoyment of the same in such a manner and such means as will leave them unimpaired for future generations."

The National Park Service employs over 8,000 full-time people, and during peak season the parks staffs are augmented by temporary workers as well as unpaid volunteers. Many RV owners and full-time travelers volunteer their time at Forest Service,

National and State Parks campgrounds – usually in exchange for their space and other amenities.

Because of the tragic events in our country on September 11, 2001, there was speculation at that time that more Americans would travel the USA, visiting national forests, parks, historical monuments and landmarks to get in touch with "their land."

Historians say that when President Theodore Roosevelt took a hard look at the devastated forests of the Eastern United States in the late 1800s he cried "Enough!" and resolved that the grandeur and magnificence of the Western landscape would not meet that same fate. He then set the wheels in motion for the creation of the US Forest Service.

Historians also report that when the friendly Chief Seattle acquiesced to the settlers' encroachment upon tribal lands in 1853 he simply cried. Indigenous peoples of the Northwest Territory believed that only the Great Spirit truly owned the land.

USDA Forest Service History

1876 – The Department of Agriculture appointed Dr. Franklin B. Hough as the first national forestry agent.

1881 – A Division of Forestry was established. Hough, in charge, continued his studies of America's timber and timber products.

1886 – Dr. Bernard E. Fernow formally took charge of the Division of Forestry.

1891 – March 3, the Forest Reserve Act created "forest reserves" without authority to hire personnel to manage the reserves.

1897 – The Organic Act allowed forest reserve management hiring.

1898 – Gifford Pinchot replaced Fernow, and managed the 60 employees.

1905 – President Theodore Roosevelt created the USDA Forest Service. Pinchot named Forester or Chief.

1911 – The Weeks Act permitted acquisition and restoration of land in the name of the American people.

USDA Forest Service Quick Reference Contact

- Camping Reservations – 1-877-444-6777 or www.reserveusa.com
- Fall Color Hotline (Sept. to Nov.) – 1-800-354-4595
- Wildflowers in Bloom Hotline (April to August) – 1-800-354-4595
- Official Forest Service Website – www.fs.fed.us
- Directory of all National Forest Campgrounds and Our National Forests magazine on-line – www.ournationalforests.com
- Public Land Recreation Websites – www.recreation.gov, www.publiclands.org, www.Int.org, www.smokeybear.com, www.millenniumtrails.org

USDA Forest Service Camping Ethics

- Use established sites. Avoid stress to an area. Leave it better than you found it.
- Stay on good ground. Stay more than 200 feet away from clean water sources, on level ground without plant life. Avoid erosion from your tent or camping group.
- Observe campfire rules. Use backcountry camping stove powered with butane or propane fuel. If you must build a campfire, collect dead and downed wood during daylight. Use established fire rings or burn on top of a mound of sand or rocky soil.
- Leave it natural. Pick up your litter. Put rocks back where you found them. If you used a wood fueled fire make certain it is completely out. If it was not an established fire ring, scatter the cold ashes and excess wood. Scatter needles or brush over the site. Take a step back. Does it look as though humans have been there?

Other information you'll want to know

- Driving off designated roads and trails is illegal in many forests. Be informed regarding the latest travel regulations and conditions.
- Check at local ranger district offices for recreation area maps, rules and regulations.
- Cell phones can save your life. You may be charged for time and equipment to find you in the event you get lost in the woods.
- In 1999, the federal government spent $591 million to fight fires that burned 605,000 acres in the USA. Careless people who start fires may be billed for the expense of putting out the fires they started.
- Individual states manage fishing and wildlife resources on forest lands. It's your responsibility to know about regulations and licenses.

Two roads diverged in a wood,
And I –
I took the one less traveled by,
And that has made all the difference.

"The Road Not Taken" – Robert Frost

2

TRAVELING ALONG THE FAMILY HISTORY TRAIL

Genealogy, family history research and memoir writing currently prove to be helpful tools for millions of Americans in the pursuit of their ancestral roots. Everyday people are traveling to destinations they previously ignored, passionately following a thread of their lineage.

There comes a time in our lives when our family heritage has meaning. We didn't want to hear about "the good or not so good old days" when we were growing up. Generally, we become interested when we realize relatives who would be our resources are aging, dying or have failing memories.

Whatever my motivation, when I reached my sixties I knew if I didn't hit the family trail soon no one else would do it. I'm at the end of the line on my father's side of the McDonalds, and have traced my ancestors from Mexico, Maine, to West Lake Ainslie, Cape Breton, Nova Scotia, and as far back as the Isle of South Uist, in the Highlands of Scotland.

From the roots of the Clan Donald there grows a mighty tree with many branches. Just when you think you've got a good lead on your family lineage you may discover you are barking up someone else's family tree. There are lots and lots of Mac and McDonalds (all Scottish) on the high roads and the low roads of the Highlands of Scotland, throughout the many Isles, in Canada and the United States.

Requests for information from my relatives had reached a dead end. And so, at the prompting of my family history writer friend, I went to the Mormon Family History Center in Beaverton, Oregon, and to begin my search.

When my mother died I acquired some family documents: my father's birth certificate and my mother's baptismal record. I took the information about my father's and my grandmother's obituary from 1960, with me to the Mormon center. In my grandmother's obituary there were Mac and McDonald, and Mac and McDougall members of the family listed. I haven't solved the mystery as to why it is one way or the other. Some say one is Irish and the other Scottish, but that doesn't seem to be the case.

I made note of the address and phone number for the Oxford County Clerk's Office in Maine, where I thought my father's birth was registered. They advised me to contact Mexico, Maine, where he was born. The clerk in the town of Mexico was helpful in finding and mailing a number of documents that gave me further clues.

She sent me copies of my grandparents' death certificates, as well as birth certificates for my father and his siblings. My grandparent's death certificates gave me the place of their birth in Cape Breton, Nova Scotia. My grandfather was born at West Lake Ainslie and my grandmother was born at Craignish. I was pushing hard on my research because I was leaving for England and Scotland in two months. I don't recommend that sort of a time crunch.

I went to the Internet and pulled up all the McDonalds and McDougalls in those towns where my grandparents were born. It was like Smiths in New York City. I wrote to the Provincial Records of Nova Scotia in Halifax. They provided me with census information for 1867, 1870 and 1887-1903. Those records verified that John McDonald and Christie McDougall were counted as individuals in the first two censuses, and together in the last. I knew my father was born in the United States in May of 1903, so I concluded my grandparents left Inverness County prior to that. My father was the first American born in that family.

The Archival Assistant in the Manuscripts Division for Inverness County suggested I look into church registers and other resources, for which she provided a list of professional genealogists available at an hourly rate. I chose the church records search, and called the Catholic Archdiocese in Halifax for information. The priest in Halifax advised me to call the pastors at Craignish and West Lake Ainslie. When I called the pastor of St. Mary's at Mabou (where records for the smaller parishes were kept) he gave me the name of Josephine Beaton, a woman in that parish who did family history searches on request. She came highly recommended. Time was running out, and the rest was done by phone and fax.

Josephine's quick search of church and county records produced the information I needed before I left for Scotland. There was a string of MacDonalds, MacDougalls, and MacPhersons on the branches of the Scottish family tree. John MacDonald was a native of the Isle of South Uist and had come to Prince Edward Island, Nova Scotia, and from there to West Lake Ainslie, where he acquired a large tract of land in 1814. From that date to the present, Josephine gave me a running list if ancestors that ended with my mother and father and their two children, of whom I was the sole survivor.

I left for Great Britain as planned. After spending several days in London, I flew to Glasgow, rented a car and drove into the Highlands. Driving on the left side of the road, with the steering wheel on the right was a new experience. I stayed at quaint bed and breakfasts along my route to the Isle of Skye. I spent the night of my birthday on Skye. I took pictures of the brilliant sunset through the dining room window while I ate.

Later, the cold wind whistled outside my second story bedroom, and the dark sky was laden with stars. Gratefully my hostess had placed a hot water bottle under the covers for my feet. I was up early the next morning to catch the 1½ hour ferry boat ride. I was first at the dock and slept on the ferry. Then there was the drive from North Uist to South Uist, over narrow roads and waterways.

Upon reaching what I thought was the end of the Isle of South Uist, I inquired at a hotel that appeared not to be ready for guests, for a place to stay. I said that I was tracing my McDonald ancestry. The young man attending the desk said, "Sure, I'm a McDonald, and that fellow over there with the paintbrush is a McDonald, and the one behind the bar is a McDonald. Most everyone on this isle is a McDonald." For some reason I didn't feel very much at home. I was overwhelmed with McDonalds and hadn't a clue which ones might be related, if any.

I stayed at an inn by the sea, where I was one of very few guests. The next day was "Mothering Day," a Sunday, (the US equivalent of Mother's Day) and many families came to the inn for dinner. I walked among the stones and shells, and tried to imagine what it was like for John McDonald to pack up his family and leave his homeland in the early 1800s. It must have been a gray, misty day, steeped in sadness – and hope for a future in a new country, Canada, in North America, across this very same ocean and so very far away.

Six months later I went to Cape Breton, Nova Scotia. With Josephine as my guide, we visited dusty Inverness County archives and ancient cemeteries, and poured over church records. We drove out to West Lake Ainslie and went to the church service. When I talked to a few people after Mass we discovered we were all McDonalds, but different branches of the tree. We searched among the cemetery headstones without finding any links to my past. In the Inverness County Archives we found my great, great, great grandfather's last will and testament, leaving parcels of land to his children

As best we could tell, my grandfather was a fireman on a locomotive, working on the laying of the railway through Cape Breton. When the railway was finished, he and his wife, his siblings and cousins, headed for the State of Maine. If they had any land at West Lake Ainslie, they probably sold it to go to the United States. I know, they all settled near each other in Maine and some in the Boston area. And, I know most of the rest of that story.

What did I learn? The search is the better part of the trail and the travel. What we see along the way is well worth noting, because there really isn't a final destination on the family history search.

The detours, those times we spend barking up the wrong tree, are often as delightful as anything else. Also, searching has become much easier and more productive, with genealogy societies, family history sections in libraries, software and Internet web sites (enter the word genealogy on any search engine), as well as increased interest and awareness.

The trumpet of a prophesy!
O, Wind, if Winter comes,
Can Spring be far behind?

"Ozymandias"
Percy Bysshe Shelley (1792-1822)

3

PLAY BALL! IT'S SPRING!

Standing at my father's side, with our right hands over our hearts, we waited for the end of the public address system's screeching of the National Anthem at Briggs Stadium. We waited for those magical words, "Play Ball!" My excitement, anticipation, and wide eyes, watched the Detroit Tigers' starting pitcher throw that first ball toward the batters box. "Is it a strike, a ball, an infield hit, or a long ball to center field?"

I was only nine or ten, but thoroughly hooked on the game, and on my team. I knew all the players' names, positions, batting averages and the team's won/lost statistics. I cut out the back of the Wheaties, Breakfast of Champions, cereal box when a Detroit Tiger appeared. Like a true Tigers' fan, I hated "them damn Yankees."

I grew up, had a family, moved to California, and the Detroit Tigers took a bleacher seat on my list of things to care about. Then, in 1981, I met a friend from Detroit for a vacation in Florida. As we came back from the Florida Keys we drove up to a local baseball stadium in Lakeland. The Detroit Tigers were in spring training. We watched about an hour of the practice session, and drove on. It's one of those memories, like standing at attention waiting for the "Play Ball!" announcement, which sticks.

During the spring of 1999, my avid sports fan, soon-to-be husband, and I were traveling in his Roadtrek 190 RV throughout the Southwest United States. We planned our trip so that we could be in Arizona during the opening of spring training, and catch an exhibition game if possible. We weren't sure which teams and players we would see. I knew it wouldn't be the Detroit Tigers in the Cactus League.

The spring training schedule wasn't out before we left Oregon in November. I ran out a copy of the previous year's schedule to get some idea about timing. Later, I would go back to the web site, or we would be there. By way of example, the previous year the Colorado Rockies' pitchers and catchers reported February 16 to the Hi Corbett Field in Tucson. Position players reported February 18, and full workouts began February 19. The Rockies first exhibition game at Hi Corbett was Thursday, March 1, against the Diamondbacks.

Once we arrived in Tucson, we picked up a list with maps and times for practice sessions in the area. When we got to the field we were given rosters of players and a schedule of exhibition games, with ticket purchase information.

We were at the Hi Corbett Field, watching the Colorado Rockies rookies and stars batting, pitching and catching. Players, manager, and coaches catered to the fans, posing for candid shots, signing bats, balls or anything presented to them for their autograph. Kids, young and old, waited with gloved hands outside the fenced areas, to catch balls heading their way.

After checking the schedule of exhibition games, we decided to buy tickets for the Cubs vs. Mariners opener in Mesa, Arizona. We were amazed at how Mesa has been turned into a baseball town. It wasn't easy finding RV space, but we did find a spot for the one night. It would have been wise to plan ahead.

The stadium was packed. We saw Sammy Sosa play a couple of innings. The purpose of the spring training is to give the rookies coming up from the minor leagues a chance to show what they can do. Some of the Mariners (our team) stars each played a couple of innings. We left at the beginning of the seventh inning because we were sitting in the sun and it was time to move along.

Most of the time it's fun to hit the open road without scheduled stops. But, for baseball fans who want to see their favorite teams in training or exhibition games, and need a space to park an RV, planning ahead is recommended. Here are some planning tips:

1. The best source of information is *Spring Training Magazine*. Go to their web site at www.springtrainingmagazine.com. This site provides a list of teams in the Grapefruit and Cactus Leagues. The Grapefruit League trains in Florida and the Cactus League trains in Arizona. Click on your favorite team for training sites and maps, as well as game schedules, ticket information, and ballpark maps. Most MLB club web sites offer restaurant and hotel information.

2. RV sites, now that's something you have to research on your own once you know where you're going to be. RV space can be at a premium near game sites. Some RV parks may have shuttle buses to training and game sites. You may wish to check city bus routes and schedules as well. Many people already travel to these exhibition games every year. Loyal Cubs, Tigers, Indians and others from all over the country prefer the warmer climate in winter.

3. For other attractions in the area, contact the local tourism bureau in plenty of time to get your requested information by return mail. Here are some of the other web sites for pre-season and regular season team information: www.sports. yahoo.com, www.sportsline.com, www.cnnsi.com, www. majorleaguebaseball.com, and. These web sites are more interesting during regular season when you can access current statistics, lineups and detailed news reports.

4. Remember, to get a head start, you may have to make your plans based on the previous year's schedule and locations. However, you will have a good idea where your team will play, and know where and when you can access the final schedule. You can always contact the team headquarters for the most up-to-date information.

Never again do you have to wait for opening day of the regular season to "root, root, root for the home team." Now, you can just drop by a spring training camp or catch an exhibition game while traveling the highways and byways of the sunnier states in winter.

MLB Spring Training History Highlights

The Arizona Cactus Spring Training League hosts National League Clubs: Brewers, Cubs, Diamondbacks, Giants, Padres and Rockies; and American League Clubs: Angels, Athletics, Mariners and White Sox.

The Florida Grapefruit Spring Training League hosts National League Clubs: Astros, Braves, Cardinals, Dodgers, Expos, Marlins, Mets, Phillies, Pirates and Reds; and American League Clubs: Blue Jays, Devil Rays, Indians, Orioles, Rangers, Red Sox, Royals, Tigers, Twins and Yankees.

Where and when spring training happens hasn't always been so well organized.

During the 1930s nearly all major league baseball players and rookies reported for spring training in either Florida or California. Exceptions were teams playing as far south as Mexico City, Puerto Rico, and Havana, Cuba. Others scattered among southern states.

The Arizona Cactus League had its beginnings in 1945, when the Cleveland Indians persuaded the New York Giants to join them for spring training in Tucson. It would be more than 10 years later before there was a major league baseball franchise club west of St. Louis. The Grapefruit League dates back to 1914.

The westward movement for spring training camps began in 1903, when the Chicago Cubs went to Los Angeles. Then, two years later to Santa Monica. They bounced around the country until their stint in Pasadena from 1917 to 1921.

William Wrigley Jr., the chewing gum king, bought into the Cubs in 1916, and later bought into Catalina Island property 26 miles off the coast of California. As a result of his influence, the Cubs held spring training on the Island from 1921 to 1951. After several years of bad weather the Cubs chose Mesa, Arizona – where they still train, and draw crowds.

In 1907 the New York Giants headed for Los Angeles. Followed by the Chicago White Sox in 1908. The Boston Red Sox trained at Redondo Beach in 1908, and the White Sox moved to San Francisco for 1909-1910.

Although the Detroit Tigers hosted the Pittsburgh Pirates in the first Phoenix, Arizona, spring training game in 1929, they remain loyal to Lakeland, Florida, and the Grapefruit League.

*The Native American believed
that the Great Spirit resided in the center of the earth
and that 'Big Medicine' fountains were the special gift from The Creator.
Even during tribal battles over territory or stolen horses it was
customary for the sacred 'smoking waters' to be a neutral zone where
all could freely be healed.*

Hot Springs & Hot Pools of the Northwest (and Southwest)
Marjorie Gersh-Young

4

GETTING YOURSELF INTO HOT WATER – EXPLORING NATURAL HOT SPRINGS

While sailing throughout what he thought was the eastern part of the world, Ponce de Leon searched for the legendary Fountain of Youth in the Bahamas, and later thought he had found it in what is now St. Augustine, Florida. These mythical magical waters were intended to make old people young again, and heal all kinds of illnesses.

Ponce de Leon had sailed in 1493 on Christopher Columbus' second voyage to America. In 1508 he conquered Puerto Rico, and then became governor of that island. Still struck by wanderlust and stories told to him by native inhabitants of the conquered territories, Ponce de Leon again set sail in search of the marvelous fountain.

The Indians actually were repeating an ancient European legend told them by the explorers. The Europeans believed the Water of Life, found in the Garden of Eden, existed in the Far East. The early Spaniard explorers believed America was in the Far East, thus natives became Indians.

In some ways most people still search for mythical and elusive fountains of youth to stay young and feel good. Unlike Ponce de Leon, who supposed by drinking the waters one would recapture youth, many modern day travelers and explorers, seek healing and soothing thermal hot springs waters for soaking away tension and worry, as well as muscle ache and joint pain.

If you are so inclined, you may travel to St. Augustine and sip from the fountain at the spring marked by the Spanish explorer in 1513, when he claimed the land for Spain. To date, history has not recorded any age regression at the site. However, if you're looking for natural "healing waters" for soaking your tired body, help is on the way.

Many years ago, I began my treks to Carson Hot Springs Resort, east of Stevenson on the Washington side of the Columbia River Gorge. This was my favorite get-away from the stress of work and a busy life in Portland. As two or three of my daughters grew older, I introduced them to the hot springs adventure. Sometimes it was a birthday treat.

In the early 1900s, river boats brought vacationers to the resort for rest, relaxation and the healing waters. Not much has changed, except people now arrive by motorized land vehicles.

The funky old 1901 St. Martin's hotel has rooms upstairs as well as cabins, and a restaurant with tasty, healthy food. The hotel lobby is where you register, check in for overnight RV parking, pay for hot tub soaking and massage, and get your assigned times. While you wait, there's plenty of cold spring water to drink, rocking chairs, overstuffed furniture and a giant checkerboard to pass the time. Or, you may prefer a walk on the wooded river trails.

When Harry and I began traveling together, we took his Roadtrek RV and hooked up in the Carson Hot Springs RV lot. After registering, we entered separate bathing facilities and soaked in old claw-foot tubs filled with hot water from the natural springs. After the soak we entered our separate, darkened quiet rooms with rows of cots and mummified bodies. There, we were wrapped as tight as we wanted to be with blankets, to sweat inside our own cocoons. My favorite spot is near the door looking out to the woods along the river, so I can feel the cool air across the uncovered part of my face.

Then, if you are into total relaxation and really want to feel like a wet noodle, you go for the massage. Many commercialized hot springs offer a full range of body pampering.

Hot springs may not be for everyone, but we have visited dozens of natural and commercialized thermal springs throughout the western United State over a four year period. When we were on the road, most often I first looked at the hot springs directories to plan our route and take advantage of those with RV parking. We used Marjorie Gersh-Young's books, *Hot Springs & Hot Pools of the Northwest* and *Hot Springs & Pools of the Southwest.* Each of these books contains over 900 listings from 13 western states, Canada and Baja (Mexico). A list of other hot springs guides accompanies this article.

According Gersh-Young, "there is nothing more enjoyable than to soak in a hot spring in ideal conditions. To me this means a beautiful pool with water at 104 degrees cascading over the rocks out in the middle of the forest at the end of a moderate hike." And, she gives credit to Jayson Loam, "the original creator of these hot springs books over twenty years ago. At that time he did the initial field work."

Only a third of the 1,600 springs listed by the National Oceanic and Atmospheric Administration proved accessible and acceptable to the researchers and contributors of these books. Some of the springs dried up, some were on private land, and others were at resorts since closed.

One well-known American discovered the healing waters so beneficial that he founded the Georgia Warm Springs Foundation for the treatment of victims of polio.

In August of 1921, at the age of 39, Franklin Delano Roosevelt (FDR) fell into the water while sailing near New Brunswick, Canada. He became chilled, and within a few days could not walk. In 1924, prior to becoming president, FDR began spending several months each year swimming in the pool of warm mineral water at Warm Springs, GA. Two years later he bought the springs, facilities and 1,200 acres of land around them. Later, with friends, he established the Foundation to provide low-cost treatment for other polio victims.

The Warm Springs water is a steady 88 degrees and gushes from a source nearly a mile below the top of Pine Mountain. Native Americans, or Indians, had long before used these springs as a place of neutrality to wash and rest their tired or wounded bodies.

Hot springs, or thermal springs, come from deep in the earth and generally occur in areas of faulted and folded rocks, where there has been volcanic activity. Some hot springs, such as in Yellowstone National Park, produce boiling water that shoots into the air in geysers. Many of the resorts in Palm Springs and Desert Hot Springs, California, have drilled individual wells to bring the water to the surface.

During our first six years on our way to Mexico for the winter, we spent a few days to a week at the Catalina RV Spa in Desert Hot Springs, to soak away in their large therapy pool. While in Mexico, we have traveled 50 miles south of San Felipe, Baja Norte, over a terrible pot-holed road to reach the hot springs in Puertecitos. There, the geothermal water bubbles up from under the rocks along the Sea of Cortez. These natural pools can get up to 110 degrees, and are usable a few hours each day during low tide.

On our way back to Oregon from a winter in Mexico, we stopped at Bailey's Hot Springs and RV Park five miles North of Beatty, Nevada, on US Highway 95. There, the natural artesian hot springs bubble up through the gravel bottom of two historic bath houses built in 1906 by the Tonopah & Tidewater Railroad.

One of the buildings has two private soaking pools, and the other hosts one large pool. Keys for the pools hang on a post. Soaking is available 8 AM to 8 PM, $3 per person for 30 to 40 minutes. Unlimited soaking is included with overnight RV parking. The temperature ranges between 98 and 105 degrees, or "hot, hotter and hottest," according to Sixto, the Aztec/Apache Native American from Palm Springs. He had managed Bailey's since 1994 for the two women owners.

Hanmer Springs, New Zealand South Island

As we traveled north on Highway 395 we stopped in Lakeview, Oregon, to check on the Perpetual Geyser at Hunter's Hot Springs Resort. During construction of a sanitarium in 1923, drilling struck a geyser that still spouts 50 to 75 feet into the air every few seconds. The sanitarium came and went, as have resort owners. New owners have reopened the restaurant, lodging and hot springs pool.

Our last overnight RV stop on the way home to La Pine, Oregon, was Summer Lake Hot Springs on Highway 31, north of Paisley. This historic bath house was built in 1927, and was known as "medicine springs" to Native Americans long before the cowboys and settlers came.

Archaeologists determined there was habitation at the hot springs more than 9,000 years ago. Four springs on the 143 acre property range from 118 to 109 degrees. Water entering the soaking pool from one of the springs is cooled and maintained around 102 degrees.

Nearly 500 years of change has occurred since Ponce de Leon sought the healing waters to restore youth. Generations of explorers, conquerors and settlers have harnessed much of the world's resources and wilderness, bringing the marvelous calming benefits of many hot springs under protective as well as commercial umbrellas. As seekers and soakers, we appreciate the access to well-maintained commercialized soaking pools, as well as the more primitive hot water spots, wherever they may spring up.

Hot Springs Books

Hot Springs and Hot Pools of the Southwest and *Hot Springs of the Northwest* Jason Loam's Original Guide(s) – by Marjorie Gersh

Hot Springs – by Stephen Hunter

Hiking Hot Springs in the Pacific Northwest (3rd edition) – by Evie Litton

Touring Montana and Wyoming Hot Springs – by Jeff Birkby

Enchanted Waters: A Guide to New Mexico's Hot Springs –by Craig Martin

Beautiful Spas and Hot Springs of California – by Melba Levick

Umbrella Guide to Northwest Natural Hot springs – Tom Stockley

Colorado's Hot Springs (2nd edition) – Deborah Frazier George

Touring California and Nevada Hot Springs – by Matt C. Bischoff

Touring Arizona Hot Springs – Matt C. Bischoff

Hot Springs of Nevada – George Williams

Everyone's Guide to Hot Springs of Western Washington – by Jesse W. Love

Hot Springs of Western Canada – by Jim McDonald, Glenn Woodsworth

Spas and Hot Springs of Mexico – by Mexico Mike Nelson

Forest Service Maps and Warnings

When you plan to hike or camp in wilderness areas it is recommended that you check in with the nearest US Forest Service Ranger Station to let them know where you are going and how long you will be there. Maps, permits, information about water pollution, and other good advice are available at Ranger Stations. An example of a US Forest Service warning from Gersh-Young's book follows:

Caution – Natural Hot Springs

- Water temperatures vary by site, ranging from warm to very hot...180 degrees F.
- Prolonged immersion may be hazardous to your health and result in hyperthermia (high body temperature).
- Footing around hot springs is often poor. Watch out for broken glass. Don't go barefoot and don't go alone. Please don't litter.
- Elderly persons and those with a history of heart disease, diabetes, high or low blood pressure, or who are pregnant should consult their physician prior to use.
- Never enter hot springs while under the influence of: alcohol, anti-coagulants, antihistamines, vasodilators, hypnotics, narcotics, stimulants, tranquilizers, vasoconstrictors, anti-ulcer or anti-Parkinsonian medicines. Undesirable side affects such as extreme drowsiness may occur.
- Hot springs are naturally occurring phenomena and as such are neither improved nor maintained by the Forest Service.

People who work together will win,
whether it be against complex football defenses,
or the problems of modern society.

– Vince Lombardi

5

FOOTBALL FANS LOVE TAILGATING

Long before most of us even thought about owning a recreational vehicle, travel trailer or motor home, there were pickup trucks and station wagons dropping their tailgates and bringing out the sandwiches, chips, sodas and beer in the stadium parking lots of their favorite college football teams.

Today, parking lots at most football stadiums have a designated area for RVs and motor homes. If parking spaces are assigned and lined then it may work best to park at the end of a row where you can roll out the awning and set out chairs. Sometimes parking space is tight and sometimes more generous.

Rule number one is to arrive early and get the best possible space you can. This becomes the meeting and gathering place for friends and family before the game, during half-time if there is time, and after the game to clean up, snack, watch the post-game report on your TV and wait for the traffic to let up.

Tailgating with a RV allows you the ultimate comfort, regardless of the weather. And, tailgating at a major college bowl game when your team wins BIG has to be the ultimate sports experience.

And so the story goes. Harry and I returned to California, on December 2, 2001, after a month in Australia and New Zealand. The next day we were heading south in the RV when I started calling family members on our cell phone. My daughter-in-law, Jan asked if we were interested in attending the Fiesta Bowl in Tempe, Arizona, to see the University of Oregon and the University of Colorado. Wow! It took us about three seconds to say yes.

The major bowl game, according to the College Bowl Championship Series (BCS bowl selection) was in Pasadena, but for loyal Duck fans the BIG game was in Tempe. The previous year Oregon State Beavers rolled over historically powerful Notre Dame's Fighting Irish at the Fiesta Bowl. That was before the BCS Championship Bowl in Pasadena. And, there's still a lot to be said about BCS picking Nebraska for the number two spot against the indisputably number one Miami for the 2002 Rose Bowl NCAA National Championship game.

For the benefit of some fans of college football, the Bowl Championship Series, or BCS, replaced the Bowl Alliance in an effort to create a National Championship without playoffs. BCS is run by commissioners from six major conferences (Big Ten, Pac Ten, ACC, SEC, Big 12 and Big East) and the Notre Dame AD.

What's old? Before 1998, bowl games extended invitations independently of each other, usually based on conference affiliations, and often before the season was completed. Frequently, deserving teams were left out of the loop. To be clear, big money is involved in the process. Advertising dollars for the rights to broadcast certain games provide treasure for college athletic departments of the participating teams. The financial interest is a point not to be taken lightly.

What's new? Computers pick the top performers based on information input from a complex and elaborate rating system that still is undergoing changes. The four bowls currently involved in the BCS process are Rose, Sugar, Orange and Fiesta. One bowl hosts the National Championship game on a rotation, sequential basis. For more NCAA football game schedules or BCS information, go to one or more of the following:

www.collegebcs.com,
www.sportsaction.com,www.espn.go.com,
www.sportsillustrated.cnn.com/football/college,
or your favorite football team's web site.

An interesting bit of irony was the fact that the Fiesta Bowl (Friday, January 3, 2003) was the major bowl game, hosting the top two BCS team picks from the 2002 season. Leaving the question for us: Can the West Coast – meaning Oregon – show up for a third year?

It took a few more years, but we did go to another bowl game on January 1, 2010 in Pasadena, when the Oregon Ducks lost to Ohio State at the Rose Bowl.

As soon as we're certain one of our Oregon teams will go to a BCS bowl game that interests us, we contact family or friends who hold season tickets and have bowl game tickets allotted. At the same time we check online for hotel options. When we were taking our RV to games the options were different.

When we went to the Fiesta Bowl in Tempe, Arizona, we drove our RV up from Mexico and spread out in the parking lot for a tailgater. When we went to Pasadena to the Rose Bowl we had the advantage of our GPS and cell phones to make connection with my son Tom and family where we all parked on the golf course near the stadium.

It would have been great to have a GPS to get us back to our car in the dark of the night. All golf paths looked the same. Many of the cars were gone. Once we found our car the trip back to the hotel was easily guided by our GPS – the traveler's friend.

He that invents a machine
augments the power of a man
and the well-being of mankind.

Henry Ward Beecher (1775-1863)

6

AIR SHOWS COMING TO LOCATIONS NEAR YOU

Ever since the Wright Brothers first awed crowds with their flying machine and ushered in the airplane age in 1903, men, women and children have been stretching their necks and shielding their eyes from the sun or glare at air shows throughout the world.

Several years ago my retired military husband and I traveled throughout the Southwest, stopping at RV parks on military bases whenever they were conveniently located and had space available. That year we saw practice sessions for the Navy Blue Angels and the Army Golden Knights Parachute Teams, and toured the Air Force Thunderbirds' museum.

During the years we drove the RV south to our winter home in Mexico we stayed at the El Centro Naval Air Facility RV Park. At seven in the morning we woke to the sound of jets overhead, circling, practicing their touch-and-go exercises and heading out for team sport. Although the Blue Angels are stationed in Pensacola, Florida, they practice their routines from early January until they open their air show season at El Centro, generally the first Saturday in March. Scheduled appearances in the United States, Canada, and abroad are listed on www.airshows.com.

U.S. Navy Blue Angels

At the end of World War II, the Chief of Naval Operations, Adm. Chester W. Nimitz, ordered the establishment of a flight demonstration team to showcase naval aviation. The Blue Angels debuted June 15, 1946 at Craig Field in Jacksonville, Florida, introducing their trademark Diamond Formation with the Grumman F-6F Hellcats.

The first flight leader, Lieutenant Commander Roy "Butch" Voris named the Blue Angels after reading about New York City's famous nightclub in the *New Yorker* magazine.

The Blue Angels' mission is to "enhance Navy and Marine Corps recruiting efforts and to represent the naval service to the United States, its elected leadership and foreign nations." Their flight demonstrations are choreographed refinements of skills possessed by all naval aviators.

Each season more than 15 million spectators are awed by the four-plane Diamond Formation, in concert with fast paced, high performance maneuvers of its two Solo Pilots, in addition to the renowned, six-jet Delta Formation.

U.S. Air Force Thunderbirds

The United States Air Force (USAF) Thunderbirds open their air show season in March. And, finish in November for their homecoming at Nellis Air Force Base, Nevada.

In 1947 the Army Air Corps gave way to the creation of the U.S. Air Force as a separate service. Six years later their official air demonstration team, designated the 3600th Air Demonstration Unit was activated at Luke AFB, Arizona on May 25, 1953.

The first training squadron commander at Luke was Maj. Dick Catledge. His left and right wings, respectively, were twins Bill and Buck Patillo. The brothers, both captains, had performed with the Sky Blazers, a USAF/Europe demonstration team for three years. Other pilots were selected from the Saber Dancers, a predecessor to the Thunderbirds.

The unit's adopted name "Thunderbirds" was influenced by the strong Indian culture and folklore of the southwestern United States where Luke AFB is located in Arizona.

According to the www.nellis.af.mil/thunderbirds, their naming comes from an "Indian legend that speaks of the Thunderbird with great fear and respect. To some it was a giant eagle…others envisioned a hawk. When it took to the skies, the earth trembled from the thunder of its great wings. From its eyes shot bolts of lightening. Nothing in nature could challenge the bird of thunder, the story said, and no man could stand against its might. The story of the Thunderbird was repeated voice-by-voice, across the generations, until at last it assumed the immortality of legend."

For the 200th birthday of our nation in 1976, the Thunderbirds were designated as the official United States Bicentennial Organization. For that year the numbers on the planes' tails were replaced by the Bicentennial symbol. The Thunderbirds are distinguishable from the Blue Angels by their white bodies accented with the black and red Southwestern Indian design related to the legendary bird.

U.S. Army Golden Knights Parachute Team

Perhaps a lesser known, but no less spectacular, member of the U.S. military's trio of air show performers, may be the Army's Golden Knight Parachute Teams. Annually, the team performs more than 27,000 jumps before an estimated 12 million people.

In 1959, the Strategic Army Corps Sport Parachute Team formed to compete in the Communist dominated sport of skydiving. They performed so well that on June 1, 1961 the Army officially recognized and activated the team. A year later the team adopted the nickname Golden Knights.

According to information on their web site "golden" refers to their reputation for bringing home medals from skydiving competition, and "knights" refers to the fact that they have "conquered the skies" and are champions of principle and conquest. Their mission includes excellence in their air show performances to the purpose of promoting the Army's success in national and international competition, and the opportunity to test and evaluate equipment and techniques.

Having won more than 400 national championships and over 60 world championships, they say that "when the Golden Knights show up to a competition, everyone else is battling for second place."

Home for the Golden Knights is the "Home of the Airborne," Fort Bragg, North Carolina, where 90 soldiers are trained in one of the Army's military occupational specialties and train with the team for three years. The black and gold parachutes and uniforms identify the Golden Knights as they seem to float out of their gold and black plane.

The black and gold teams perform two different shows, the Full Show and the Mass Exit. Both shows begin with one jumper exiting the aircraft at 12,500 feet and tying in the American Flag. The first jumper becomes the narrator on the ground for the remainder of the show, which consists of a baton pass in air, a demonstration of how to deal with a parachute malfunction, tandem jumps and formations in the air, and colored smoke coming out of their shoes.

Sgt. Maj. Michael R. Deveault is quoted on a web site as saying, "The Team demonstrates skill, esprit de corps, team cohesion and discipline. We also represent the Army Values and are role models to all."

Are you in the mood for an air show? Do you want to show your support and appreciation for the Army, Navy, Marines and Air Force? Do you want to see the best of the best performances in the air? Then go to www.airshow.com, and pull up air show schedules for Blue Angels, Thunderbirds, or Golden Knights, and get out the sunglasses and binoculars.

Many of life's failures
are people who did not realize
how close they were to success
when they gave up.

Thomas Edison

7

HISTORICAL PERSPECTIVE ON CARS

Thomas Alva Edison was born Feb. 11, 1847, in Milan, Ohio, the youngest of seven children. Following three unsuccessful month of irritating the teacher with his constant curiosity and questions, his mother, a former school teacher, began his homeschooling.

Best known for the invention of the electric light and the phonograph, Edison patented more than 1,100 inventions in 60 years. After 10,000 attempts with a storage battery failed to produce the electric light he said "Why, I have not failed. I've just found 10,000 ways that won't work."

On the golden anniversary of the electric light Henry Ford moved Edison's original Menlo Park, NJ, laboratory to Greenfield Village, Ford's huge museum near his childhood home in Dearborn, Mich.

Ford, a contemporary of Edison, was born in 1863. He became a machinist in Detroit and completed his first gasoline engine in 1893. With the success of his Model T, Ford began profit sharing with his employees.

In the very fewest of words – "My, how far we've come." Electric lights and automobiles are everywhere. Along with all that accompanies the results of the curiosity of two geniuses who welcomed the industrial age.

Born and raised in the suburbs of Detroit, I have been to Greenfield Village, numerous times. Ford and Edison were names we knew well. The other day I was discussing Motown with friends. I informed them that the name for the musical explosion came from "Motor town." Detroit. The original recording studio was located on Grand Boulevard – or what once was called mansion row. Detroit has seen good and bad times. But the hard working factory workers have, for decades, kept the wheels of our cars on the roads of America and many other countries.

At a July Fourth Parade here in La Pine the history of cars came back to me in the form of the old "Army Jeep" and other "war" vehicles. I was reminded of the gap in production of automobiles when the factories switched, almost overnight, to the production of Army jeeps and trucks, tanks and munitions. American and Canadian auto plants became important production centers from 1939 to 1945.

During World War II, in the 1940s, gasoline was rationed, because everything went to the war effort to support our troops. My father worked for a bakery. Getting bread on the tables of the people in the Detroit area was important, so he had a high priority sticker.

Backing the car out of the driveway was a major, calculated event for my parents. I did a lot of walking and taking public transportation.

According to my World Book, "Soon after the United States entered the war in 1941, American car and truck production for civilian use slowed and then almost stopped. Fewer than 223,000 cars were sold in 1942, and only 139 in 1943. U.S. auto plants produced more than 2,600,000 military trucks, over 600,000 jeeps, and more than 49,000 tanks."

After the war, Europe recovered rapidly and manufacturers began to adopt the American assembly line approach to auto production. West Germany soon ranked second to America in automobile production. The German-made Volkswagen became the biggest hit of all times. And, by 1957 the U.S. imported more cars than it exported.

During the 1980s, when I went back to Detroit to visit family and friends, I was quizzed about the make of car I drove. Honda, I answered, but, I added, it was assembled in Ohio. I haven't been back to Detroit for several years, and my answer today is that I am a proud owner of a Subaru. You don't see as many Subarus in all of Detroit as you see in Bend, Sunriver and La Pine, Oregon

Much as I would like to support the U.S. auto industry, I opted for better gas mileage, quality and economy back in 1998. By the time I'm ready for my next car the people in Detroit may have dealt with the gas-mileage issue.

With the wars in Iraq and Afghanistan running longer than expected we are paying higher prices for gas and it isn't rationed at the pump – yet.

I pledge allegiance to the flag
of the United States of America
and to the Republic for which it stands,
one Nation under God, indivisible,
with liberty and justice for all.

World Book Encyclopedia, 1967

8

OH, GOD, I LOVE THE USA – PLEDGE OF ALLIGENCE

For many years I have received emails from irate individuals who concentrate on one phrase of the pledge of allegiance that children recite, or used to recite, at the beginning of each school day. I suggest we prayerfully meditate on each word and phrase of our pledge as citizens to see how we measure up.

I appreciate my *World Book Encyclopedia* and my old *Dictionary of Thoughts*, because, that is where I always find what I want and need. Again, I went in search of a required reading that impressed me as a high school student. That short story is "The Man without a Country," an 1863 lasting literary effort by Edward Everett Hale, a Unitarian clergyman, author, editor and humanitarian.

Philip Nolan, a young army officer in Hale's story, said at his court-martial that he wished he would never hear of the United States again. He then was put on a ship and the crew was given instructions that Nolan was never to be given any information about his homeland. Before he died he begged for reconciliation with his country.

The "Pledge of Allegiance" came a few years later. Public school children first recited the pledge as they saluted the flag during the national School Celebration held in 1892. President Harrison called for patriotic exercises in schools to mark the 400th anniversary of the discovery of America.

The original pledge was written by the associate editor of the *Youth Companion*. The National Flag Conferences of the American Legion expanded the original wording in 1923. In 1942, Congress made the pledge part of its code for the use of the flag. In 1954, Congress added the words "under God."

When we attend ceremonies in Mexico, citizens place their hand over their heart and recite their pledge. I don't understand Spanish, and I am a visitor in their country, so I stand in respectful silence – as I would in any other country not my own.

Summertime brings out the flags, parades, and patriotism in the United States because of Memorial Day, Flag Day, Fourth of July and Labor Day. Any excuse for a long weekend and a picnic.

At our house, we fly the American flag during the summer. I have three comfortable Old Navy T-shirts with American flags on their fronts – one kaki color 2003, a blue one 2004, and a white shirt for 2010 – that I frequently wear around the house and into town.

The other day I was cleaning out a cupboard and found two old American flags, triangle folded. I called the La Pine American Legion Post #45 and talked to Pat Cotton. He said to bring old flags there for ceremonial burning. They don't have a schedule for the ceremony, but probably will do one in July if they have accumulated some old flags.

I have, on occasion, witnessed a ceremonial, military or American Legion flag folding ceremony, and asked for a copy of the words spoken by the Women's Auxiliary of the American Legion Post #45 when they fold the large flag into a triangle. Their words follow:

"The point of honor of the flag of the United States is a canton of blue containing the stars representing the states our Armed Forces served in uniform. The point of honor of the flag of the United States dresses from the left to the right and the only time it is inverted and displayed in the manner in which you see it today is when it comes to serve as a pall on the casket of a veteran who has served their country honorably in uniform.

"In the evening, in the Armed Forces of the United States during the ceremony of Retreat the flag is lowered and folded in a triangle fold, and kept under watch throughout the night as a tribute to our Nation's honored dead. The next morning it is brought out at the ceremony of Reveille and run up aloft as a symbol of our belief in the resurrection of the body.

"The first fold of our flag is a symbol of life.

"The second fold is a symbol of our belief in the eternal life, and this fold we make in honor and remembrance of the veteran whom we are commemorating today, for they too gave of a portion of their life for the defense of our country and our flag, and we are here today to perform this flag-folding ceremony in order to show forth to their family and friends that their efforts to attain peace throughout the world have not been in vain and shall never be forgotten.

"We fold to the left in the shape of a triangle, for this is where our hearts lie – and it is with our hearts we pledge allegiance to the flag of the United States of America, and to the Republic for which it stands – one nation under God, indivisible, with liberty and justice for all.

"We fold again to the left in the shape of a triangle, representing our weaker nature, for we, as American citizens, trust in God, and it is to Him we turn in times of peace, as well as in times of war, for His divine guidance.

"We fold to the right as a tribute to our Armed Forces, for it is through these same Armed Forces that we protect our country and our flag from all her enemies, whether they be found within or without the boundaries of our Republic.

"We fold again to the right as a tribute to our country; in the words of the immortal Stephen Decatur, 'our country, in dealing with other countries, may she always be right; but it is still our country, right or wrong.'

"We fold to the left in tribute to the one who entered into the valley of the shadow of death, that we might see the light of day, and this fold is made to honor Mother for whom it flies on Mother's Day.

"We fold it again to the left as a tribute to our womanhood; for it has been through their faith, love, loyalty, and devotion that the characters of the men that have made this country great have been molded.

"We fold it to the right as a tribute to Father, for he, too, has given of his sons for the defense of our country since she was born.

"We fold from the stripes toward the stars; for, whereas the stripes represent the thirteen original colonies that founded our Republic, they are

now embodied in the fifty sovereign states represented by the stars, so that the stars cover the stripes.

"We fold to the right in the shape of a triangle; for, in the eyes of a Hebrew citizen, this represents the lower portion of the seal of King David and King Solomon, and glorifies in their eyes the God of Abraham, the God of Isaac, and the God of Jacob.

"We fold again to the left in the shape of a triangle; for, in the eyes of the Christian citizen, this represents an emblem of Eternity and glorifies in their eyes God the Father, God the Son and God the Holy Spirit.

"When our flag is completely folded, the stars are uppermost, which reminds us of the national motto: "In God We Trust."

"After the flag is completely folded and tucked in, it takes on the appearance of a three-cornered cocked hat, ever reminding us of the soldiers who served under General George Washington, and the sailors and marines who served under Captain John Paul Jones, and followed by their comrades and shipmates in the Armed Forces of the United States, having preserved for us the rights, privileges and freedom which we are enjoying today."

Thanks to the La Pine American Legion Post #45 for providing me with a copy of the above "Anonymous" Flag Folding Ceremony text used by the women's auxiliary. And, thanks to the volunteers who place the American flags on the downtown streets of La Pine prior to Memorial Day. It is a beautiful display of our nation's colors.

Who can repay
those who have lost loved ones in combat?
What on this earth
can compensate for the loss of life?

Dennis Smith, sculpture
Living Memorial Sculpture Garden
Weed, California

9

LIVING MEMORIAL SCULPTURE GARDEN HONORS THOSE WHO SERVED

Each Memorial Day and Veterans Day, names of honorably-discharged veterans, living or dead, are added to the marble-clad Hot LZ Memorial Wall at the 132-acre Living Memorial Sculpture Garden (LMSG) nine miles north of Weed, California. Currently there are over 1,000 names engraved in the marble.

For a donation of $100 to the LMSG, you can honor your vet for his or her military service. My husband Harry Taylor and I were deeply moved on our first visit to the LMSG. With his permission, I had his name engraved on the Hot LZ Memorial Wall in honor of his 26 years in the U.S. Air Force.

Hot LZ refers to a Vietnam combat loading zone. A sculptured helicopter tops the memorial, and a bronze plaque honors Ace Cozzalio, "one of America's great combat pilots, and important founding member of the LMSG."

The LMSG, at the northern foot of Mt. Shasta, honors all veterans and military personnel. It is on USDA Forest Service land and was founded by a group of veterans, supported by the

Weed/Lake Shastina Kiwanis Club. For more information, go to http://LivingMemorialSculptureGarden.org.

Dennis Smith, Marine Corps veteran and artist, says, in the LMSG brochure, "Each sculpture has personal meaning for me in terms of life experience and personal incidents. Through the arts we have the means to peacefully consider violence and to ask questions as well as offer possible solutions."

Smith's giant metal sculptures are described as symbolic, intimate, patriotic and moving. The garden's 132-acres, with one-way access roads, provide an opportunity to drive-by, park, or walk closer and reflect.

Korean War Veteran Monument at LMSG

The Why Group was the first sculpture installed in the LMSG and is central to the questions we all ask about war. As Dennis Smith asks, "After all the deeds are done and the soldier goes back home, sits alone in front of a warm fire on a cold night having time to think his own thoughts he may ask himself a few questions. Why me? Why not me? Why him and not me? Why war? Why not war?"

Having been to the Vietnam Memorial Wall in Washington, D.C., we found Smith's sculpture of the POW-MIA soldier in a cage a gripping portrayal of how it was. According to a story by Dick Sumner posted on the web site in 2000, the USFS supplied 80,000 Ponderosa Pines to be planted by volunteers. Developers of the LMSG said they hoped that over 54,400 would survive, representing lives lost in Vietnam.

Other moving representations of the drama and the sadness of war feature: *The Flute Player, Those Left Behind, The Peaceful Warrior, Korean War Veteran Monument, Coming Home, and The Nurses. The Greatest Generation* sculpture honors veterans of World War II, based on Joe Rosenthal's famous photo of the second flag raising on Mt. Suribachi on the island of Iwo Jima, February 23, 1945. *The WIA* (Wounded in Action) is the most recent sculpture, displaying severed limbs.

The Living Memorial Labyrinth can be the first or last thing your experience at the entrance/exit of the LMSG. The labyrinth is "A memorial path for all. Walk in peace. Remembering and healing." And the plaque on the stone entrance sign reads as follows:

A place to remember where we have been;
A place to remember what we've been through;
A place to remember those faces so well of friends and loved ones;
A place to remember, a place to mend;
To bring our minds back, to reality again,
To help us see our futures, so we can move on.
Jim Leach – LMSG Founder

If history repeats itself,
and the unexpected always happens,
how incapable must man be of learning from experience.

George Bernard Shaw (1856-1950)

10

LIFE'S HISTORY LESSONS

Prior to graduating from high school I took a moderate academic interest in history and geography. It was troublesome being tested on dates, names and places, where and when historical events occurred. In concentrating so hard on the details I lost interest in the broad scope of the events.

The summer of my eighteenth year, following graduation, I traveled by car with my parents to my grandparents' farm in Pennsylvania, down to Washington, DC, then on to Philadelphia, New York City, Boston, and my other grandparents' home in Mexico, Maine.

We went to the Smithsonian Institute, the Lincoln Memorial and Washington Monument. I stood in the rotunda of our nation's Capitol building, walked around the outside of the White House and on the Capitol Mall. On a hot summer evening we listened to the U.S. Navy Band playing on the steps of the Capitol building.

The following day when I stood in Independence Hall in Philadelphia and listened to the sound of voices simulating the discussions that took place in that hall it gave me chills. Days later I went to the top of the Empire State Building, walked the streets of Manhattan and viewed the Statue of Liberty from across the Hudson River.

Then we visited Boston Harbor where the rebels made their statement leading to independence from England, and freedom from domination by a foreign power across the Atlantic.

That summer, my very wise parents, showed me how to experience history. Since that time, travel is synonymous with learning history.

I took one semester of community college. Then I quit college for eight years to get married and have a few children. After 22 years of going to night classes off and on, and finally a very full senior year at Portland State University, I was granted a bachelors degree in general studies, arts and letters.

While taking History of Western Civilization 101, 102 and 103 once a week for three terms, I had a marvelous instructor who brought history to life. His exuberance always prompted me to sit two rows back to avoid the spittle spray. However, that's when I began to put world history and world events into place.

One of the first courses I took upon returning to college was Political Science. I tried to gain a better understanding about how the political process and governmental processes worked. I first voted for president when we all "Liked Ike." I lived in Michigan which had an open primary, so I didn't have to declare a party until I moved to California.

This I know, there is a huge difference between running for office and serving in an office. The primary elections are literally all over the political party map in terms of dates, methods and outcomes. The General Election is the real deal. I still don't understand the Electoral College, or how the Supreme Court got involved in the 2000 election, but I'm not alone in my confusion.

I'm 75, and met a real president for the first time, Sunday, May 11, 2008, when William Jefferson Clinton was campaigning for his wife in our area. And, I have the pictures to prove I was there.

Return to Washington, DC

The first year of our marriage, Harry and I drove out of Mexico in late March, heading for Florida to see family. We were making 300 to 400 miles per day in the RV to get to Naples before his son, my daughter and our grandchildren left my daughter Mary's house to go home to Alaska. We crossed through several southern states with brief stops.

Following that visit we trekked up the Atlantic coast, stopping at every major point of interest until we reached Washington, DC. It was Earth Day 2000, and Leonardo de Caprio was hosting a major event on the Capitol Mall. It was Harry's birthday, and I took him to lunch at the Smithsonian.

Harry showed me parts of the Capitol he remembered from his four-years at the Pentagon. We stayed at Andrews AFB, and were there the Elian Gonzales' father was flown in from Cuba to pick up his son, who had been brought to the Capitol from Miami.

We attended Easter vigil services at the National Catholic Basilica of the Immaculate Conception. The Shroud of Turin traveling display was in the crypt of the church. Our timing was exquisite. That evening we had all the pomp and circumstance anyone would wish for.

And, we returned to the Capitol again in 2010. We had been in Egypt for more than ten days. On our return to JFK New York airport we rented a car and drove down to Harry's hometown in North Carolina for a few days. On the way back to New York, we spent three days in Washington, DC. We rode the rapid transit from the Andrews AFB area to the Capitol. We sat in the gallery of the House and of the Senate. We took the on-off tour bus all over the area. We paid our respects at the Arlington National Cemetery, visiting John F. Kennedy's final resting place with its eternal flame.

Generally, I prefer to go to new places where I've never been before. However, Washington, DC, our national treasure, is an exception to that rule. Our Nation's Capitol is forever new, and a great source of pride. I appreciate all that has gone into making our Capitol what it is today. I appreciate all the effort that goes into maintaining our national treasure. All politics aside, the Capitol is the seat of the government of the people who live in the land of the free and the home of the brave. Long may she live.

What's in a name?
That which we call a rose
by any other name would smell as sweet.

"Romeo and Juliet"
William Shakespeare (1564-1616)

11

WHAT REALLY IS IN A NAME?

When I tell people my father was born in Mexico, they get that startled look on their faces. Then, I add – Mexico, Maine.

The State of Maine has several cities named after foreign places. I recall seeing post cards with mileage directional signs from Augusta, Maine to places like Norway, Lisbon and Mexico.

When I moved to California from Michigan I mispronounced the name of the city of La Canada. When I moved to Oregon from California I mispronounced Willamette for the river in Portland. Many of the California city names are in Spanish, because they were there first, and named for saints because of the missionaries moving from south to north. Portland, Oregon was named after Portland, Maine by the flip of a coin. It could have become Boston, as in Massachusetts.

New England is obviously where the British staked out their first claim, and Nova Scotia was obviously where immigrants from Scotland settled in the "new world," now known as Canada. La Pine is named for a single tree near the state park and Bend is named for a kink in the Deschutes River.

Many of the original territories, states, counties, and cities were named for the explorers, discoverers, Native American indigenous tribes or peoples, settlers, or founders. All these names mean, or have meant, something to the people who live within their particular boundaries.

Weed? Over the many years I have passed through Weed, California, where Highway 97 and the Interstate-5 come together I have mused "What a strange name!"

A few years ago on our return from Mexico to La Pine, Oregon – we stayed in a small RV park in beautiful downtown Weed. We walked the streets of Weed and discovered a charming city, and ate great spareribs from the outdoor smoker.

According to the 2000 census there were 2,978 people, 1,184 households, and 747 families residing in Weed. The city was incorporated January 25, 1961, and boasts that it is a "clean, safe, attractive rural community…a friendly town where visitors are always welcome to share the beauty, culture, and creativity that this community nurtures and supports."

The city gets its name from Abner Weed, founder and local lumber mill owner. In 1897 he bought the Siskiyou Lumber and mercantile Mill and 280 acres of land, that is now Weed, for $400. A bronze stature of Abner Weed stands sentry at the artistic town square or town corner. It's worth a walk on the main street to see the murals on the sides of buildings.

According to Wikipedia (online encyclopedia): "People of Weed have so far been patient with tourists, amused by the town's name, due to the fact that "weed" is also slang for marijuana." Tourists often contribute to the town's economy, buying souvenirs bearing the town's name.

Discontent is like ink poured into water,
which fills the whole fountain full of blackness.
It casts a cloud over the mind,
and renders it more occupied about the evil which disquiets
than about the means of removing it.

Owen Feltham (1602-1668)

12

THE TRIP THAT NEVER HAPPENED – 9/11/2001

Airline tickets purchased, hotels arranged, car rental waiting, ready to introduce my husband Harry to my school chums and walk with me into memories of my youth and young adult days. We looked forward to my 50-year high school class reunion in Michigan. I had included a trip to Mackinac Island and lunch at the Grand Hotel.

We drove up from La Pine the day before our flight to stay with my daughter Tina. She lives in Vancouver, WA, and dropped us off at PDX by 6:00 AM the morning of 9/11. We took care of the preliminaries and waited at the gate, boarding passes in hand, for the call to board our flight.

When we came to our terminal I noticed a crowd of people standing near the snack bar watching the television. We bought a newspaper, and Harry was reading the sports page when I went to see what was on the TV. There was footage of smoke billowing out of a tall building. Everyone speculated that a private plane went off course.

It wasn't until the chilling live broadcast of a second plane hitting the other tall building with the same results that I interrupted

Harry's reading to tell him what I just saw. Then I went back to the TV and saw the Pentagon hit. I knew that would get his attention because he spent four years at the Pentagon.

The announcement to turn in our boarding passes came next. We went to the airline ticket counter and asked about rescheduling. No one knew yet how serious a situation we were in. We couldn't rebook. I called my daughter and she told me where I could find a key to the house. Then we arranged transportation to her house. The rest of that day and night was spent watching the television coverage of the disaster, making phone calls to cancel hotels, car rentals, and flight charges. We prepared to go back to La Pine the next morning.

Usually we hear planes while at my daughter's. The sky was silent except for the planes from the Portland Reserve Air Base – circling the area. We were stunned by the entire chain of events.

I called my girlfriend Ann who left Sacramento that morning and got as far as Las Vegas, when all flights were grounded. She did get out of there to Michigan in time for the reunion. And, she sent me pictures.

We quickly put everything into perspective. Although a little disappointed, my inconveniences paled in light of the thousands of people killed, families traumatized; the loss of mothers, fathers, husbands, wives, and children – from nearly every country on our shrinking world. Rescue workers, health care persons, and those who came from all over the United States to help the people of New York City were weighed down by the carnage of this unparalleled disaster.

I was sitting at my ironing board in front of the television in Glendora, California, when John Kennedy was shot in Dallas. I was in the Portland Airport, with boarding pass in hand when the Twin Towers in New York City collapsed from an attack.

Sometimes it's hard to remember, we're all children of the same God.

All progress is made by unreasonable people.
Reasonable people adapt to the world around them;
unreasonable people try to change it.

George Bernard Shaw

13

THEY WERE HERE BEFORE US

When my children were growing up we made at least one trip a year from Beaverton, Oregon, to Kah-nee-ta resort, about 18 miles east of highway 26 on the Warm Springs Reservation. Sometimes I reserved a couple of the motel rooms. That was before the casino and hotel were built on the hill. Most often we stayed in a teepee.

Once, during spring break, the snow was drifting into the teepee through the opening at the top. In the morning, there was a sprinkling of snow on the ground. After breakfast, cooked over an open-fire stove in the middle of the teepee, everyone headed for the hot springs pool to get warm.

Heading south on highway 26 onto the Warm Springs Reservation the first sight of the beautiful plateaus still takes my breath away. I can almost see the Indians on horseback riding across the rims. I respect their rights to the land they occupy and taught my children respect for the Native American's land and their rights.

While at the University of Portland in 1976-77, working on my master's degree, I chose the following thesis title: *A Study of the Interrelationship between the American Indian Movement (AIM) and the Mass Media.* That turned out to be a 200-page thesis, but

I was learning so much and had so much more to say that it was a labor of love. I have been interested in the Native Americans and their causes ever since. That thesis is now a book, titled, *Alert the Media: How the American Indian Movement used the Mass Media.*

Considering the many, many times I have passed the Museum at Warm Springs north of Madras on highway 26 – it was a pleasant surprise and worth-our-time to stop at the museum last summer.

Chief Delvis Heath of the Warm Springs Tribe has said, "Way back in the 1960s, we could see that the old ways were disappearing, the old language was disappearing, and pretty soon none of our young people would know where they came from or who they were. That's when we decided to build a museum."

Construction began on May 7, 1991, and the Grand Opening was celebrated on March 13, 1993. Total cost of the project was $7,628,900.

The stated mission of the Museum is "to preserve, advance and share the knowledge of the cultural, traditional and artistic heritage of the Confederated Tribes of Warm Springs." The Warm Springs, Wasco, and Paiute Tribes are joined to form the Confederated Tribes.

Over the Museum's entrance is carved the Sahaptin (Warm Springs) word "Twanat" – translated, to follow traditions and culture. Entering the lobby visitors will notice green floor tiles, representing the flow of the water. Great wooden pillars project the strength and vigor of the trees and enduring traditions of the people. The circular tower portrays the circle of life and a belief in the interconnectedness of all things.

An invitation to explore the past greets visitors on their self-guided tour throughout the permanent exhibition. Listen to ceremonial songs as you view petrography, such as "She who watches" on the walls. Enter into the Tule mat lodge, Wickiup, and plank house for a walk through the history. And, weather permitting, bring a picnic lunch to pause as you explore the grounds and walk the nature trail.

As we attempt to walk in the moccasins of our Native American sisters and brothers, let us remember, respect and reverence for those who were here before us. Let us be grateful to them for preserving the environment in its entire splendor as we all move on together into the future.

Words, words, words!
They shut one off from the universe.
Three quarters of the time
one's never in contact with things,
only with the beastly words that stand for them.

Aldous Huxley (1894-1963)

14

WORDS, WORDS, WORDS!

The above part of the quote is familiar to most of us, but the rest of it may not be quite so familiar. Aldous Huxley, British novelist, actually can be quoted as saying, "Words, words, words! They shut one off from the universe. Three quarters of the time one's never in contact with things, only with the beastly words that stand for them."

I wonder what Huxley might have thought about the social networking and the use of electronics to communicate with everyone, all the time.

Those of us who depend so much upon the use of words to communicate everything that pops up in our heads, to those who may or may not care, are humbled by the words of Huxley. We prefer to think that our words bring us and others closer to each other and the universe, closer to people, places and things. But, admittedly, it is a lonely road we travel, and we seldom hear from the people we try to reach through our words.

Since I first unscrambled a handful of letters in the first grade to make words, I have been fascinated with stringing these odd symbols together. That handful of tiny letters is much like the magnetic letters now used to write poetry on the refrigerator doors of America.

I have great respect for the printed word. There is something so permanent, concrete, about words on paper. Just ask your attorney about words on paper, and how meanings can change with just the dot of an "i" or the crossing of a "t."

When I first moved to Oregon in 1967, I began writing for newspapers and magazines. I joined writers' groups and attended conferences. Being in the presence of other writers always makes my road less slippery. I have subscribed to *Writer's Digest Magazine* for a very long time. A copy of "The Writer's Prayer" came into my possession in 1972, compliments of the Writer's Digest School. When I get "writer's block" or start on a new project or simply need a kick start, I read the seven-paragraph prayer. I will share the following paragraph with you.

"Help me to remember always that words have the power to destroy – or build; the power to spread ignorance – or dispense knowledge; the power to darken the world with hate – or light it with love."

Words are tiny pieces of language. While in Mexico we realize the value of language. Somehow we manage to communicate with the people there because they try harder than we do to understand us. Friends have completed interactive Spanish courses, three nights a week for 10 weeks, and received their diplomas. It takes commitment and desire to learn a foreign language. My two years of high school Latin do not serve me very well. Each year we say we will learn more Spanish. But, talk is cheap.

Meanwhile we will use hand signals, write directions and numbers in the sand, and be grateful they are so kind to us visitors. After all, it's been said "One picture is worth a thousand words." You need only see a brilliant sunrise or sunset to appreciate "being speechless."

One picture is worth 1,000 words.
(or, more than 10,000 words)

Quote masters attribute versions of this common phrase to
Either Chinese proverb or New York advertising agency.

15

ONE PICTURE IS WORTH 1,000 WORDS

I've had a camera in my hands ever since I can remember. My parents had already filled albums with photos long before I started my own adventure with photography. I realize some people care far less about documenting the times, people and places of their lives than I do. Maybe they figure I'll do it anyway and they may as well let me.

Growing up in a suburb of Detroit, Michigan, I took my camera to school, to the zoo, to the lakes on outings, to pajama parties and birthday parties, and of course, on all vacations with family or friends.

When I was 15, my parents and I had recently returned from a trip to my father's hometown in Mexico, Maine, when a fire broke out – or exploded up the smoke stacks – in the chemical factory behind our house. While we were watching from our vantage point in the back yard, and my father was trying to decide whether to move the car up the street out of danger, I finished off a roll of film in my Kodak Brownie box camera.

The Royal Oak Daily Tribune photographer arrived on the scene when the flames and black billows of smoke were less dramatic. My father wandered over to talk with the photographer and told him I had a roll of film in my camera. I kindly rewound the film and gave it to the photographer. The next day my photo of the fire was on the front page – above the fold – of the newspaper.

When I went by the newspaper a couple of days later to pick up my $5 paycheck and the 9 x 12 enlargements from my roll of film, you can bet I was all aglow and on my way to a career in photojournalism.

At the end of that year, the Tribune ran its special "Best of the Year" pictorial section – and my photo of the factory fire was on the front page – above the fold. Not only that, it was the only photo in the section by an amateur.

I kept taking pictures of family, friends, other people and lots of places. Then, in 1968, after moving to Beaverton, Oregon from California, I read a notice in the *Valley Times* for a photographer/correspondent to fill in for staffers on vacation. So, with seven children to tend to, little spare time, a few writing classes under my belt and the use of the newspaper's camera, I was back in my element and hitting my career stride.

Since that time, there have been several educational opportunities as well as career twists and turns with newspapers, magazines, corporate communications, publications and advertising.

I have been writing travel and general interest articles, columns and books since 2000, with almost all my writing accompanied by photographs.

Photographic technology has come a long way. Going from film to digital has been amazing. I spent hours scanning photos onto my computer and exporting them to flash drives. Learning that process wasn't as simple as I make it sound. I have Photo Shop but am not accomplished there.

In the past I took a box of photos with me to Mexico. I never knew what I would need for the articles. Now, I take flash drives that fit in zip-lock plastic sandwich bags.

I haven't finished scanning photos. There are so very many photos, so many memories of trips at home and abroad. I am one very fortunate woman to have lived so long, done so much, and visited so many beautiful, interesting and exotic places.

Music is the mediator between the spiritual and the sensual life.
Although the spirit be not master of that which it creates through music,
yet it is blessed in this creation, which,
like every creation of art, is mightier than the artist.

Ludwig van Beethoven (1770-1827)

16

MUSIC AS INTERNATIONAL LANGUAGE

The Cascade Festival of Music night of Broadway show tunes and pops concert was one of the highlights of our summer in Bend, Oregon. As we sat at the back on risers in the huge tent in Drake Park, absorbing the wonderful melodies, my mind drifted to other times and places where music was so special and so moving.

We were in Vienna, Austria, sitting in the concert hall of the Hofburg Imperial Palace and listening to the Wiener Hofburg-Orchestra play the Straus waltzes that were so familiar in my youth. My mother frequently played recordings, filling the house with music. Her parents came from what was the Austrian Empire in the late 1800s. She prized what she considered part of her heritage. It was awesome to be there and hear music that stirred the hearts and souls of the people of the times in which the music was written and first performed.

Hofburg Imperial Palace, Vienna, Austria

Three years later we were in Salzburg, Austria, during the Mozart Festival. There were musicians on every street corner, and in the squares. We attended an elegant Saturday luncheon concert at St. Peter's Restaurant. The following day we attended the Mozart mass at the Cathedral. An orchestra played in the four balconies surrounding the sanctuary. Soloists also appeared on the balconies, in addition to a choir of 100 voices.

In Sidney, Australia, we viewed their marvelous Opera House from the ferry boats in the bay, day and night, as well as up close. Their Opera house has several theaters and performance halls, with simultaneous performances. We opted for an evening of symphony music. The symphony hall has outstanding acoustics. Our seats were in the balcony behind the orchestra. We were provided a unique "behind-the-scenes" opportunity to observe the conductor and the audience, and to watch the seldom-seen musicians in the percussion section. Our concern about being underdressed was for naught. Many came in blue jeans or walking shorts.

In 1996, I toured Israel and Jordan with a group of Episcopalians from the Portland area. As a part of our nine month preparation for the trip we learned chants and repetitive verses so that we could be spontaneous with our expressions. While on the Sea of Galilee, the boat operators cut the motors. In the silence, we joined in song. When our group finished singing there was another boatload of pilgrims ready to respond in song. The silence and the music on that water were powerful.

I play no musical instrument but am greatly appreciative of the ability of composers and musicians to capture and organize sound into melody and rhythm. Central Oregon has wonderful musical offerings all year. We are here in the summer and try to take advantage of local offerings. One summer we attended the Jazz Festival in Sisters, and the musical "A Day In Hollywood, A Night In Ukraine" presented by the Cascade Theatrical Company in Bend.

When I married Harry in 1999, our marching in song was Louis Armstrong's "What a Wonderful World." And I say, "Amen."

Music is one of life's pleasures that we sometimes take for granted. Many people provide us with those pleasures, and each of us "march to a different drummer." We listen to what we like and appreciate what we hear. Some of the best music happens on my morning walk in the woods. I hear the birds greet the day, with some background noise from the Pine Squirrels, and an occasional breeze rustling through the trees.

Books are the quietist and most constant of friends;
they are the most accessible and wisest of counselors,
and the most patient of teachers.

Charles W. Eliot (1884-1926)

17

BOOKS AS TRAVELING COMPANIONS

Some of my best "friends" are hard-bound, others have a softer exterior, but they all are pretty much black on white in their presentations. I can accept that, their being opinionated, that is. That's what I would expect of any good book.

What absolute joy it was learning to read. In finding new friends in near and far away places. I found out how to "escape" by burying my nose in a book. I discovered the public library, with an incredible number of volumes for all ages.

When I was in the seventh or eighth grade I asked the librarian for something interesting to read. She gave me *Gone with the Wind*. Wow! I read that volume in less than five days, with the help of a flashlight under the covers at night.

In June of 1984, I began a running list of "Books Read." I have it on my computer under "Personal and Family." I haven't counted, but I suspect I have read all Sidney Sheldon, John Grisham and Philip Margolin, along with lots of best sellers, books on tape, and many non-fiction books, as well.

I have kept a daily journal in the cheap spiral notebooks since sometime in the seventies. I jot down a few notes each night, and sometimes paste in a political cartoon, family email, obituary, or something else of note. Inside the covers of my journal I record books recently finished, with author, title, and notes, and later transfer to computer.

There have been times when my husband Harry and I dispute what may have happened and when. Generally, I can go to my journal and solve the mystery. I know the dates of all our comings and goings from state to state or country to country. It only matters to me that I know where I've been, what I've seen and what books I've read.

I have two friends in San Felipe, Mexico, who have developed macular degeneration. They both have had to stop driving, and have severely decreased vision, and listen to recorded books. One is past 65 and the other is past 70. And, according to Wickipedia, "10% of patients 66 to 74 will have findings of macular degeneration. The prevalence increases to 30% in patients 75 to 85 years of age."

I have become increasingly aware of our great gift of sight, and the limitations imposed by macular degeneration and glaucoma. I want to read more books. I'm grateful that I can see the computer keys and the computer screen. Grateful that I can see the photos I have stored on my computer.

*Authors who produce writing with substance
have an almost sacred role in the word-worn world.
They are priests of poetry, prophets of perspective.
Their writing is ingested, digested, and integrated.*

"Wabi Sabi for Writers" – Richard R. Powell

18

WRITING IS AN ACTION WORD

While visiting with my daughter-in-law in Port Hadlock she brought out a gift bag for her father and me. Among the books is the one from which I have quoted. I said, "I look forward to getting to know this new friend." For me new books are new friends.

Before looking into *Wabi Sabi for Writers*, I said I was going to write my column. When asked what I was going to write about I said "I won't know until I start writing." Sometimes, that is the way ideas develop.

Then I randomly opened to a page in this new book and looked for a phrase or passage that would, as Powell says, "Take readers beyond themselves."

Truth be known, that is the place most serious writers want to go. We don't really know what drives us. But, something does drive us. Others may not try, or want to try, to understand our muse. We do what we have to do to live.

For me, living is research. I'm constantly gathering ideas and perspectives and images and sounds and feelings, and digital photos. While still a child, my mother frequently referred to my personality as "still water runs deep." It has taken me decades to understand what she knew long ago, and I was meant to discover. My thoughts take me on adventures. Sometimes pleasant, and sometimes scary. But they do take me beyond myself.

We take annual journeys on the Oregon Coast and up to the Olympic Peninsula area to visit our families. For me, travel is a thoughtful, meditative, renewing experience. Especially when we follow the coastal waters.

All who wander
are not lost.

J.R.R. Tolkien

19

NOMADS AMONG US

Tolkien wrote the *Hobbit* and the first two volumes of *The Lord of the Rings* during his tenure at Pembroke College in England. Bilbo's journey in the *Hobbit* was based on a 1911 hiking adventure Tolkien took with friends in Switzerland.

Although Tolkien's books involve exhaustive journeys or missions in search of someone or something, he spent the bulk of his life as a professor of English. So, whether you write books or read books – you never really have to leave home.

During the summers of my youth, growing up in Michigan, my mother would pry my nose out of a book to do something or other that I'd rather not be doing. I loved my local library, about a mile away, and the librarians were my friends and advisors. Although we were a traveling family – off to see my grandparents-far-away in the State of Maine or my grandparents on the farm in Pennsylvania – in books, my mind could wander to far off places anytime I wanted

Tolkien was born in South Africa, to English parents of German heritage. Aren't we all quite a mix of ancestry?

Some of my travels abroad, "across the pond" as they say on the East Coast, involve searching for my roots. When I was young, and my grandparents were alive, it didn't occur to me that I needed to know where they came from. In my 50s, I went to Scotland and to Nova Scotia (New Scotland), Canada to explore my father's lineage. In August of 2006 we traveled in Eastern Europe, and I had hoped to travel to L'vov in the Ukraine, from where my mother's parents migrated in the late 1800s. That didn't materialize because I had a bronchitis attack in Bucharest.

While in my undergraduate program at Portland State University, I took several hours of independent study on Pre-1900 Austria. I poured over maps that demonstrated the changing face of Europe over the decades before and after World War I and World War II to pinpoint the Austrian Empire location where my grandparents lived.

With the exception of the Native Americans (Indians), our ancestors all came from somewhere outside the borders we define as the United States of America. Nearly one-third of the southern part of our country once belonged to Mexico. Conflict defined the borders. There were fewer battles with our northern neighbors, and little or no redefining of our northern borders.

During a trip to southeastern Canada, we learned about historical border disputes at Niagara Falls and in Quebec. Growing up in Michigan, we learned about Canada and United States disputes. I love travel north of our border. I have roots in Canada – Nova Scotia. In the winter we live among our neighbors to the south in Mexico.

So, all who wander are not lost – they are exploring and learning about this great, big, wonderful world.

Only that traveling is good
which reveals to me the value of home,
and enables me to enjoy it better.

Henry David Thoreau (1817-1862)

20

CROSSING BORDERS

Immediately following terrorist attacks in New York City and Washington, DC, on September 11, 2001, cars at the US-Mexico and US-Canada borders were backed up for hours. Everyone wanted to go home, which ever side of the border that meant for the individual motorists.

Everything we took for granted before September 11 now requires a closer look.

Within a month of the terrorist attacks Canada announced it would spend $165 million on new anti-terrorism and security measures "including increased border security and prevention of passport fraud." Considering bomb threats and suspicious vehicles, this was good news for law-abiding citizens on both sides of the northern borders.

Crossing the Canadian border

Vehicles entering Canada may be searched at the discretion of customs officials. You may be waved through, but it's best to allow for delays and observe the following guidelines.

- Be ready to answer standard questions: "Where are you from? Where are you going? How long will you be in Canada? What is the purpose of your trip? Are you bringing anything with you that you intend to leave behind?

- Passports are not required for US citizens entering Canada. However, that could change, and do carry identification such as a birth, voters or naturalization certificate showing citizenship, and photo ID. If young children are in your party you may be asked to substantiate their relationship. (Returning to the United States is an entirely different subject. Prior to 9/11, I did a walk on to the ferry from Port Angeles, WA to Victoria Island, Canada. I traveled light with a credit card. No photo ID. I was delayed coming back to USA because I had no proof of citizenship.)

- Carry vehicle title, registration and automobile insurance card. A call to your insurance agent will clarify your vehicle coverage while traveling in Canada. If the vehicle owner is not in the party you may need to produce written permission from the owner.

- Contact your health insurer about your coverage while traveling in Canada. Generally, Medicare does not cover health care out of country.

- US citizens entering Canada may bring the following: 200 cigarettes (1 carton), 50 cigars, and 14 ounces of tobacco; 1.1 liters or 40 imperial ounces (1 bottle) of liquor or wine, or 24 x 355-milliliter (12-ounce) bottles or cans of beer for personal consumption. (subject to change)

- Firearms are strictly controlled in Canada. All firearms must be declared and registered at Canada Customs for a fee. It's the law.

- Owners of dogs or cats must have current (within 36 months) rabies vaccination certificates.

- Driving Under the Influence (DUI) conviction is considered a criminal offense in Canada. Individuals with criminal records without waivers can be refused entry.

- Your dollar may go further in Canada. For best exchange rates use your credit card or debit card for purchases, and ATMs for cash. As a visitor to Canada you can claim a refund of 7% on every dollar spent while in the country on accommodations and most goods you take home. Keep your receipts for rebates.

For additional information go to Canadian Customs or US Customs web sites. Or call Canadian Customs at 204-983-3500 or 506-636-5064, from outside Canada.

Crossing the Mexican border

Here are a few basic considerations when crossing the Mexican border. Most major U.S. cities have a Mexican Consulate with English speaking representatives willing to answer your questions. Safety is an added consideration. Border towns are the most dangerous. Being attentive to your surroundings is sensible no matter where you travel.

More and more, Canadians pass through the United States on their way to Mexico. They winter in Mexico because of the weather, and sometimes because their Canadian currency stretches farther against the peso. Canadians have additional concerns about their medical insurance coverage and their social security when they are out of their country for extended periods of time. They have limits regarding how often they cross borders, and how long they stay out of their country.

Crossing into the United States from Mexico, in the best of times, is fraught with long lines and delays, primarily in the past the concern was transport of drugs into the States. The watchdogs at the border have increased since 9/11. The US provides the Mexican government with financial assistance to patrol borders and strategically place check points along their highways and by-ways.

Border guards or military police at check points may come into motor homes out of curiosity, to see what a luxurious life on the road is like, or they may be doing what they are trained to do, look for drugs or guns. Never offer them anything that could be misconstrued as a bribe. Friendliness can be misunderstood. Just stick to the facts.

It should be emphasized that persons crossing into Mexico need to understand the laws of the country they are entering. Absolutely no firearms or ammunition. That will be the last sign you see before approaching the crossing guard station in Mexico. You may think you can get by without Mexican automobile/vehicle insurance, but if you are in an accident you are at the mercy of the Mexican officials. If you have entered into a contract to lease a lot, rent a house or purchase property you are no longer a tourist, and must have an FM-3. You may never be asked to show your FM-3, but like auto insurance you don't want to be caught without it.

You have a choice of declare or nothing to declare lines at the border. They can assess a heavy duty on any major "new" items purchased in the United States or Canada but manufactured in China or Southeast Asian countries. Use common sense in bringing goods in or out of Mexico.

A reminder, credit cards and US drivers' licenses are not proof of US citizenship. United States or Canadian passports and/or certified copies of birth certificates for all passengers are recommended. Canadians may obtain "border crossing cards" from U.S. consulates in Canada. The holder of a border crossing card can use it to enter the Untied States from either Canada or Mexico, contiguous territory only.

Rules of the road in Mexico

- Drivers must be covered by Mexican insurance. Auto accidents are considered criminal offenses in Mexico, and regardless of fault, involved vehicles are usually impounded until investigations are completed.
- An automobile permit is required when driving into the interior of mainland Mexico beyond the border cities. Permits are not required in Baja, Mexico. The permits, good for 180 days, may be obtained at the border. The vehicle's owner may pay the fee with cash or credit card. There are Federal Inspection Points located on all principal highways to the interior. Some of the major highways require a toll.
- Vehicle Title of Ownership is required. If the vehicle owner is not in the party, written permission from the owner for a specific time period must be presented. The Mexican car permit will

be stamped to that effect. Permits will be surrendered upon leaving Mexico.

- There is a little known and less understood meaning for the left-turn signal in all or part of Mexico. Get a clear interpretation of the left-turn and U-turn rules where you will be driving. For instance, when a driver behind you sees your left-turn signal flashing that tells him he can pass you. He doesn't have to slow down while you make your left turn. The safety rule is for you to slow down and let him pass you from behind, or turn off at the nearest right shoulder and make your left turn from there when traffic clears. The left-turn lanes on highways may be to the right of the traffic lane.

Re-entering the United States

The Immigration and Naturalization Service on both sides of the border for Canada, United States and Mexico continue to work together toward fair and sensible guidelines for ultimate safety and smooth passage. Expect new security measures in the future.

When re-entering the United States the burden exists for you to declare and be prepared to prove citizenship. Passports, or government issued resident passes are required for U.S. citizens returning from either Canada or Mexico, due to heightened security it is strongly recommended you be prepared to present passports. SENTRI passes issued by the U.S. Department of Homeland Security allow passage through express lanes at certain border crossings when returning to the United States. For declaration of certain food and purchased goods, it is best to check current regulations.

The Alaska Highway
winding in and winding out
fills my mind with serious doubt
as to whether "the lout"
who planned this route
was going to hell or coming out!

Retired Sgt. Try Hise, written while stationed
at Summit Lake, Historical Mile 392

21

ALASKA HIGHWAY JOURNEY TO THE TOP OF THE WORLD

Alaska, known as Seward's Folly, Seward's Icebox, Walrussia, and Icebergia when the territory was purchased from Russia in 1867, has since provided the United States with fabulous natural resources, a strategic location, and a huge bargain at two cents an acre, or $7.2 million.

Alaska was considered vulnerable to Japanese invasion following the bombing of Pearl Harbor in 1941 – Asia lies across the 56-mile wide Bering Strait. Thus the eight-month construction of a highway through Canada from the lower 48 States was considered a military necessity.

The U.S. paid for construction of the portion of highway through Canada in exchange for right-of-way. That 1,214-mile stretch was turned over to the Canadian government in April 1946, and opened to the public in 1948.

Alaska, with its 587,875 square miles, became the 49th state admitted to the Union in 1959. Dubbed the, "last frontier," Alaska is one-fifth the total area of the entire United States, and draws hundreds of thousands of tourists annually, by land, air, and sea.

The Alaska Highway begins at Mile 0 in Dawson Creek, B.C., Canada, and ends at Mile 1520 at Fairbanks. The actual end of the highway is Delta Junction, with a 98-mile stretch of the Richardson Highway to Fairbanks.

The MILEPOST is a critical guide for traveling the highway. It covers the traditional east access route to the Alaska Highway from Montana through Alberta, and the west access route from Washington State through British Columbia. *Northwest Mileposts*, a companion guide, covers U.S. interstate and other connecting highways to and through Canada. For weather and other information go to www.themilepost.com.

My husband, Harry, and I have flown to Alaska about seven times each. His son is married to one of my daughters and, they lived in Anchorage for 15 years. Harry has traveled the Alaska Highway, both directions, three times.

With the exception of one 100-mile stretch without services, you will find gas, food, lodging or RV parks every 20 to 50 miles. Not all businesses are open year-round, nor are they open 24 hours a day. Keep your gas tank half full. There are almost 100 commercial campgrounds and about 30 government campgrounds along the Alaska Highway. Reservations are recommended during the summer.

When the beauty of the scenery becomes hypnotic, it's time to stop and get out the camera or the fishing pole, go gold panning or soak in a hot springs.

Stop at the visitors' center in Dawson Creek to find the original Milepost 0 marker. Have your picture taken.

- Fort Nelson Heritage Museum, Mile 283, in B.C. has displays of pioneer artifacts and history.
- Stop at Muncho Lake, Mile 437, for a breathtaking view of the deep blue-green waters. Tour by boat, cast for trout, picnic or camp nearby. Laird River Hot Springs Provincial Park, a favorite RV spot is 40 miles further.
- Visit Watson Lake's Northern Lights Center, Mile 613, Yukon. Post a sign in the "signpost forest," started in 1942 by a U.S. soldier working on the highway.

- Whitehorse, capital of Yukon Territory, Mile 887, is headquarters for the Royal Canadian Mounted Police. Takhini Hot Springs is 17 miles north of town. Take time to tour the Yukon River through Miles Canyon.
- See ice fields, hike mountain trails at Haines Junction/Kluane National Park Reserve, Mile 985.
- Tok, Alaska, Mile 1314, is the crossroads. The Glenn Highway cutoff bypasses Fairbanks and takes you toward Palmer, Anchorage, and the Kenai Peninsula.

At Delta Junction, Mile 1422, you can purchase a certificate verifying you reached the end of the Alaska Highway, then to Fairbanks. For more adventure take the Dalton (Top of the World) Highway to the North Pole and Alaska Pipeline home, Prudhoe Bay.

From Fairbanks, take Highway 3 to Denali National Park, an entirely new adventure, where you see black bear, Dahl sheep, moose, and reindeer in their incredible environment. Allow plenty of time to take in all that Alaska has to offer on the return trip. According to Harry, "there is as much to see and experience on the way back, and you can catch what you missed on the way driving north, and take time for fishing."

In mid-summer you will have more daylight hours than you ever imagined. You will be in the vast land of the midnight sun and glaciers – everything is bigger than life, salmon and halibut are abundant, and Mt. McKinley is always snowcapped.

When driving in Yukon Territory and on certain Alaska roadways headlights are required at all times. Seat-belt use is mandatory in Alaska, Yukon and British Columbia. Watch for road construction signs, frost heaves in early spring, and beware of animals on the road, especially after rain when they like to lick the asphalt. For additional information see previous article or go to Canadian Customs or US Customs web sites.

I love snow, and all the forms
of the radiant frost.

Percy Bysshe Shelley (1792-1822)

22

EVERYDAY'S A HOLIDAY AT WHISTLER

While holiday travelers are humming "I'm dreaming of a white Christmas" we are somewhere south of the border – where it is warm and sunny.

Although Whistler provides a festive atmosphere all year, in winter it's all about snow. They have 33 lifts, with the capacity for transporting 59,007 skiers/riders per hour up Whistler or Blackcomb mountains. There are more than 100 trails on each mountain, and the longest run is seven miles. Staggering statistics, since organized downhill skiing didn't begin until 1965.

Long before boards were strapped to boots and pointed downhill on snow. Long before European explorers and settlers came to southwestern Canada, the St'at'mic people lived 25km north of Whistler around what is now Pemberton. They spent their summers on the shores of Green Lake, at what is now Whistler, where they camped, fished and gathered berries. They returned to their valley, around Pemberton, for the winter.

During the hundred years following Captain George Vancouver's 1792 exploration of the area, several expeditions sought an easier route to the Cariboo gold fields. By 1911, the Pacific Great Eastern Railway had been pushed through to Alta Lake on its way toward Prince George.

In 1914, Alex and Myrtle Philip opened Rainbow Lodge on the north-west corner of Alta Lake, with guests arriving by rail. For decades Alta Lake was the most popular summer fishing and tourist resort area west of Banff.

In the mid-1950s a group of Vancouver businessmen started looking for a site to develop for a bid to host the 1960 Winter Olympics. They settled on London Mountain, known locally as Whistler Mountain because of the whistling marmots on its flanks.

Though unsuccessful in their bid, they were inspired by the Winter Olympics at Squaw Valley, California. As a result, Norwegian entrepreneur Franz Wilhelmsen formed the Garibaldi Lift Company to explore the recreational skiing potential of the mountain. Wilhelmsen put in the first ski lift at Whistler Creek, in what is now known as Creekside, and downhill skiing began winter season 1965.

On July 2, 2003, the Vancouver-Whistler 2010 Bid Corporation realized their dream when the International Olympic Committee (IOC) voted them the host city for the 2010 Winter Games.

Whether drawn to Whistler for the snow or following Highway 99 north on the Gold Rush Trail from Vancouver to Lillooet, through Whistler, you are promised some of the most spectacular scenery British Columbia has to offer.

Hotel or RV park reservations are recommended any time of the year. Riverside is the only full-service and dry-camping RV Park in the area. They also offer year-around log cabin accommodations. The nearest Provincial Parks are Callaghan Lake, 15km to the south, and Nairn Falls, 25km to the north – without showers, hookups, or water.

There was a time when overnight RV parking or camping was permitted in the Whistler Village lots – not today. And, the rule is enforced with towing and a fine.

From Riverside, you can take a long walk over the Fitzsimmons Creek and through the woods to Whistler Village. Trails are beautiful and well marked. Maps are available and advisable. Many people ride bikes, and the wide trails are also kid-stroller friendly.

Today, summer activities in and around Whistler Mountain include canoeing or kayaking on the beautiful rivers and lakes, as well as fishing, golf, hiking, rock climbing and horseback riding. Whistler Village offers plenty of interest for children of all ages who sign up for their summer camp, or take their skate boards and rollerblades to the Meadow Park Sports Center next to the basketball court. The Village 8 Cinemas and Rainbow Theater show movies for adults as well as children. There are two swimming pools at the sports center, or picnicking and swimming at Alpha Lake park area.

Whistler, British Columbia – home to 2010 Winter Olympics events, provides a festive atmosphere throughout the year. In the summer the adventuresome take their mountain bikes up on the Blackcomb gondola and ride down one of the mountain's more than 100 trails. Including the seven mile run.

While in T-shirt and shorts, you can imagine the thrill of swishing and traversing down those Alpine slopes in winter as you watch mountain bikers two-wheel it down to the village square. It takes your breath away – watching.

As the sun sets slowly behind the mountains it becomes downright chilly in the village square because generally there is still snow somewhere. So, bring a warm sweat shirt, or buy one in the Village so you can sit outside and eat Wiener Schnitzel and mashed potatoes.

If your Canadian loop takes you along the old gold miners trail, through Whistler, Pemberton and Lillooet, then you can head toward Merritt, on to Kelowna and down the Okanogan Valley— where fruit is abundant in June, July and August.

Lodging or RV Parks at Whistler

Lodging or RV space is at a premium in and around Whistler, both summer and winter. There are 5,200 rooms at Whistler Village. Following are suggested contact numbers and web sites.

- Whistler's Central Reservations Service – Toll free: 1-800-WHISTLER; 604-932-2394 or www.mywhistler.com.
- Hotels, Chalets, Town homes, condos – Toll free: 1-877-905-4044; 604-905-4013 or www.whistlerplanner.com.
- Bed & Breakfast accommodations and other information offered through Whistler Chamber of Commerce – 604-932-5528 or www.whistlerchamberofcommerce.com.
- Riverside: Whistler's year round RV resort and campground – Toll free: 1-877-905-5533 or www.whistlercamping.com or Email: info@whistlercamping.com.
- Provincial Parks information at www.bcparks.ca:
- Brandywine Falls, 20km south of Whistler; Callaghan Lake, 15km south of Whistler;
- Alice Lake, 45 minutes south of Whistler; Nairn Falls, 25km north of Whistler; Birkenhead Lake, 54km north of Pemberton.

Other parks include: Calcheak Forest Recreation Site, 15km south of Whistler Village, 604898-2100; Dryden Creek Resorts, 45 minutes south of Whistler, 877-237-9336; Klahanie Campground & RV Park, 1 hour south of Whistler, 604-892-3435; Paradise Valley Campground, 12km north of Squamish, 604-898-3678; Cedar Bend Campground, 4.3km north after Pemberton, 604-894-3322.

*Travel is fatal to prejudice,
bigotry, and
narrow-mindedness.*

Mark Twain

23

SEE POINT ROBERTS, WASHINGTON VIA BC, CANADA

The modern day, curious traveler shares common interests with the explorers of old who crossed continents and massive bodies of water to see what was "over there." The difference is that we seldom go anywhere without a map – they were charting new courses for civilization.

While we waited in the car line-up, and I was navigating our summer trip across the Canadian border at Blaine, Washington, I noticed the southern most tip of Vancouver, British Columbia on the map was a different color. The magnifying glass revealed that Point Roberts, below the 49th parallel, is in Whatcom County, Washington.

Point Roberts can be accessed by land via a 23-mile drive through Canada, crossing the international border at Tsawassen – or by sea to the 1,000-boat-slip marina at Point Roberts.

After crossing the border we headed down the B.C. Delta and found an RV camp next to the Splash Down theme park. The following morning we headed south to the border, again. It was July 14, and Tsawassen had streets blocked off for its annual

Tour de Delta bicycle races. We detoured, bought a newspaper and coffee, and watched some of the racers zoom by.

There is no delay crossing into or out of Point Roberts. Most of the cars there bore Canadian license plates, and the boat slips were full.

Americans who live in Point Roberts and work on the Washington State mainland are looking at four border crossings each workday. NEXUS lanes (special permits for those who apply and are approved) at the Peace Arch at Blaine, Washington have been expanded to give frequent-crossing members 13 hours a day of expedited access.

According to the Point Roberts web site, they enjoy "a tremendous amount of sunshine and 40 percent less rainfall than that of Vancouver and Seattle.

"Popular activities in Point Roberts consist of hiking, strolling along the beach, watching Orca whales, seals, birds, and fishing. Boats can be chartered from the Marina and bicycling/walking trails are also available."

The AAA Tour Book for British Columbia points out, "Boundary Marker Number 1, the last remaining original marker from the 1857-62 survey, stands in a park at the west end of Roosevelt Road. Lighthouse Marine Park on Marine Drive at the southwest end of the Point, features a 600-foot boardwalk and an observation deck offering views across the Strait of Georgia to Vancouver Island and the Gulf Islands."

Point Roberts Golf and Country Club as well as the Point Roberts Marina Club, and natural beaches keep residents and visitors satisfied that they have made the right decision to spend their time and money in this small community.

There is lodging at Maple Meadow Bed and Breakfast, Sunny Point Resort and Whalen's RV Park. In addition to the Marina and Country Club, food is available at Brewsters Tavern and Restaurant, The Reef, TJ's Grill, and the South Beach House Restaurant.

For the curious traveler, go to *All Point Bulletin*, the newspaper of Point Roberts, Washington and Delta, British Columbia. Not a major tourist attraction, PR is very interesting because of its location. Sometimes we go places just to say we've been there.

Twas the night before Christmas, when all through the house
Not a creature was stirring not even a mouse;
The stockings were hung by the chimney with care,
In hopes that St. Nicholas soon would be there.

Prof. Clement C. Moore (1779-1863)

24

KRIS KRINGLE LIVES IN LEAVENWORTH, WASHINGTON

Father Christmas, St. Nicholas, Santa Claus and Kris Kringl all show up on cue among the twinkling lights, horse-drawn carriages, roasting chestnuts, strolling carolers, and aromas of sugar, spice and all foods nice in Leavenworth, Washington.

This festive Bavarian Village, nestled in a beautiful valley surrounded by mountain peaks that rise to more than 8,000 feet, welcomes more than a million-and-a- half visitors each year. Because of popular demand, the well-attended Christmas Lighting Festival in December now includes Sundays.

On Fridays, the town is dark, awaiting the Saturday lighting festivities. At dusk on Saturday everyone gathers at the gazebo in the center of town to sing "Silent Night" and witness the transformation of the village as thousands of twinkling lights turn it into a winter wonderland.

Busloads of tourists, recreational vehicle travelers, and cars with the young and the young at heart come to Leavenworth to experience and share the warmth, love and Christmas spirit.

For details regarding bazaars, events, activities, concerts, lodging and dining during the Christmas Lighting Festival go to: www.leavenworth.org.

But, if you can't make it to the Christmas Lighting Festival you can experience all the same festive energy throughout the year. In January there is an Ice Fest; February hosts the Annual Chicks on Sticks Race; April has the Leavenworth Choral Festival and Ale Fest and; May provides a giant Maipole for the Maifest parade and dance. In June you have your choice of the Bavarian Bike & Brews Festival, the Leavenworth Wine Walk, or the Leavenworth International Accordion Celebration. July offers Icicle Creek Chamber Music Festival and Kinderfest & Fourth of July Celebration.

Throughout the remainder of the summer you will have the opportunity to experience the Acoustic Music Festival, Leavenworth Wine Tasting Festival, the Fall Music Festival, Wenatchee River Salmon Festival, and the festivity that first brought people and notoriety to the village – the Washington State Autumn Leaf Festival.

A Little Bavarian Village History

Homesteaders came to Leavenworth in 1885, settling on the Icicle Flats. By 1890, Settlers were moving into the Chumstick Valley and around Lake Wenatchee. They were farming and mining for precious metals. Big changes took place when the Great Northern Railroad completed its line through Leavenworth in 1892 and over Stevens Pass in early 1893.

In the 1920s, the town lost its sawmill, and the railroad was rerouted to the valley. The town was hit hard by the Great Depression and then World War II. In the 1950s, a handful of people started looking for change. Ted Price and Bob Rodgers, owners of the Squirrel Tree Restaurant at Coles Corner, along with Owen and Pauline Watson, owners of Alpen Rose Inn, turned to the University of Washington's Bureau of Community Development for help.

After a year-long study they initiated the Autumn Leaf Festival in 1964, and began a major facelift for the town. In time, more and more of the old buildings were remodeled in the Bavarian style.

Leavenworth Nutcracker Museum, open May-October, claims over 4,500 different kinds of nutcrackers on display. At the Kris Kringl shop it's Christmas all year long. A sold-out summer theater goes into November and December. The Icicle Creek Music Center features classical chamber programs, jazz, Latin and acoustic music throughout the summer. Art in the Park downtown has artists' displays from May through mid-October.

This small Bavarian Village offers something for everyone, all ages. Don't forget Mardi Gras and the Oktoberfest – and always bring a hearty appetite when you visit Leavenworth.

How to get there

From Everett head east to Highway 2, past Snohomish, Skykomish, and over Stevens Pass. During the winter months you may encounter snow on the pass. Check road conditions. According to the people of Leavenworth, "It's always dry and almost always sunny in Leavenworth."

From the waterfall he named her,
Minnehaha, Laughing Water.

"Hiawatha" – Henry Wadsworth Longfellow

25

WATER, WATER EVERYWHERE

Since 1967, I have been stopping at Falls Terrace Restaurant when traveling I-5 between Portland and Seattle, or other points north. While traveling south one summer we stopped at Falls Terrace to meet friends for lunch.

Much to our surprise when we finished lunch we took a stroll through the Tumwater Falls Park. Although I had been in the park before I never had made the loop all the way around the park. Big, old Dogwood trees were in full bloom, an awesome sight. An old man with his cane, parked on a bench, watching and listening to the water falling over an edge in the river.

Many years ago, the Saturday morning *Oregonian* ran an article and photo showing the frozen Multnomah Falls in the Columbia River Gorge. An enlarged photo of that sight hangs in our bedroom. I've traveled the scenic Columbia River George road dozens of times, stopping at each of the falls along the way to Multnomah Falls. But only once have I seen the falls frozen. It was a trip worth taking.

Niagra Falls, U.S. side viewed from Maid of the Mist boat.

In 2005, we spent a day at Niagara Falls, Ontario, Canada. As a child, I traveled with my parents from Detroit through Canada, crossing at the falls into Buffalo and on to Maine. I remembered the noise, the roar of the rapids and the massive waterfall. I remember getting wet from the mist. In '05 we took advantage of going under the falls and on the Maid of the Mist.

Sometimes it is worth taking some extra time to explore areas we think we know. Been there, did that, but forgot to buy the T-shirt.

Because our friends live in the Olympia area they were quite familiar with the little known Tumwater Falls State Park treasure. There are spectacular waterfalls throughout the United States, and in every country we have visited in this wonderful world. It pays to take time to smell the roses, and walk the new and the old pathways of life, and pause to listen to the power of water tumbling down cliffs and ledges.

For my part,
I travel not to go anywhere,
but to go.
I travel for travel's sake.
The great affair is to move.

"Travels with a Donkey"
Robert Louis Stevenson

26

OREGON SCENIC HIGHWAY 97 – THE ALTERNATE TO I-5

From 1843 to 1869, between 250,000 and 500,000 emigrants set out from Independence, Missouri for the Willamette Valley in the Oregon Territory. The 2,000-mile trip took from five to six months for those pioneers fortunate enough to survive and make it all the way to Oregon City.

Today's travelers can drive the approximate route in less than two weeks – and have plenty of time to stop at interpretative centers along the way to get the full story, pick up maps, literature, and a flavor of what it was like to pioneer.

Ox-drawn, covered wagons once rumbled along that part of the Oregon Trail that is now Interstate 84, where the Columbia River separates Washington from its neighbor to the south. Many of those early travelers became road weary and awestruck by the beauty of the area. Most put their wagons on rafts and continued the journey on the Columbia River. Others started detouring and settling on the north and south sides of the river where Biggs, Oregon and Goldendale, Washington now dot the map.

By 1770, emigrants were following the John Day River southwest of Baker City. Two and a half miles west of the river the trail forked.

The right fork was the primary route that ultimately arrived at the Biggs settlement on the Columbia River. The left fork was the cutoff to the Barlow Trail. There were many Oregon Trails.

In 1853, Celinda Hines wrote in her journal "...went two miles from the river...dry camp...we came to two roads, one leading to the upper and the other to the lower ferry of the DeShoots (Deschutes) river. We took the lower road because the river is sometimes fordable at the lower ferry."

Today's snowbirds with their covered wagons (recreational vehicles and homes on wheels) move up and down Highway 97, seasonally, between Canada and California. Passing through Washington and Oregon they prefer scenic Highway 97, taking time to enjoy the outback and byways while avoiding the traffic and fast pace of Interstate-5,

When Canadians, Washingtonians, Alaskans and those who have been summering in the north cross the Columbia River in late summer or autumn, on their trek south, they follow a portion of the Biggs branch of the pioneers' wagon trail. The small hamlet at the junction of Interstate 84 and Highway 97 is named for William H. Biggs, an early settler and legislator. It was a stopping place for travelers and a shipping point for wheat.

Heading south you pass through – or visit – Wasco, Maro, Grass Valley, Kent, and hopefully stop at Shaniko, where you will be provided with a self-tour map of the "ghost town." Once a thriving sheep sheering, wool storage and shipping center, Shaniko boasted a large warehouse that could hold four million pounds of wool and all the wheat available at that time.

The Shaniko Museum (where you pick up your map) was once the cloakroom attached to the front of the Bakeoven School. Later, the Shaniko School House was built in 1901 for $2,000. For 15 years it was a two-room, one through eight grades school, then a high school with the first class graduating in 1921.

The Shaniko Historic Hotel, located one block off Highway 97, first opened in 1901 as the Columbia Southern Hotel – "the finest hotel in all of Central Oregon." All the rooms and baths are upstairs. Rooms are named in memory for some of the Wild West's lesser known residents and heroes. The first floor served, alternately, as a hotel lobby, dining room, bank, department store, lunch counter, bar room, and dance hall.

After a night's rest you can continue on down Highway 97 toward Madras in Jefferson County – home to Native Americans from the Warm Springs Reservation, and nearby Kah-Nee-Ta Resort and Casino. Here you will see the county's namesake Mount Jefferson, as well as other mountains, rivers, forests, open plains, lakes and rolling farmland.

If you pull off at the Ogden Wayside along the Crooked River you will have several breathtaking views of deep ravines, railroad and automobile bridges, and a distant ribbon of a river. The park is named for Peter Skene Ogden, 1793-1854. He was an important early fur trader, and Ogden, Utah also bears his name.

In the fall of 1825 Ogden led a Hudson's Bay Company trapping party on the first recorded journey into Central Oregon. He was in the Crooked River Valley again the following year, bound for the Harney Basin and the Klamath Region, where he discovered Mount Shasta.

Now, take time to see Smith Rocks up close, even though you get a good view from Highway 97. Follow the signs at Terrebonne to Smith Rock State Park, stretch your legs along one of the many trails, or watch the young and daring rock climbers scaling their favorite cliffs.

Check your travel directory for space as you pass through Redmond and approach Bend, Sunriver and La Pine. And, if you brought your woods and irons you will find some of the most spectacular golf courses in the country. Schedule a shopping trip in downtown Bend or at Costco, lunch at the Pine Tavern, coffee at one of the many strategically located Starbucks, or a picnic in Drake Park to watch the ducks at play.

Don't be in so much of a hurry that you forget about the High Desert Museum, just south of Bend's city center. The High Desert, according to the museum's literature, is also known as America's Outback, and "covers one-fifth of the Continental United States and includes the rugged and sparsely populated expanse from Southern British Columbia through Nevada's Great Basin and from the Rockies to the Cascades and Sierra."

The High Desert Museum is part zoo, and offers indoor and outdoor exhibits, animal habitats and nature trails. Take time to browse in the Silver Sage Trading museum store and eat at the Rimrock Café.

Now you are entering the Newberry National Volcanic Monument, ten miles south of Bend. You will see signs directing you to Lava Lands Visitor Center, Lava Butte, Lava Cast Forest and Lava Caves. We hear that the early astronauts sometimes practiced moon walking on this rocky terrain.

You may not have noticed you've been following the Deschutes River since you left Madras. So, if you haven't been rafting and shooting the rapids, or playing a round of golf at one of Sunriver's finest courses – you may be ready to take a side trip. Signs lead to Paulina and East Lakes located inside the Newberry Crater, favorite fishing holes. As you turn off Highway 97 you will soon see a visitor's center where you can pick up maps and literature. Golden Age passes are good at the gate. Take the trail up the slick, black Obsidian Flow, and see why the Native Americans used this glass-like substance for their arrowheads.

Before you get to La Pine, if you are camping or traveling in a recreational vehicle, you may want to call and reserve space. You have a choice of the RV Park on Highway 97, or the Thousand Trails RV Park a few miles west of the highway, or check out the La Pine State Park out the State Recreation Road.

Native Americans have always lived and traveled throughout Central Oregon, however, the first Europeans were trappers and fur traders who came to the area in 1830. The La Pine area was first explored in 1843, when John C. Fremont's exploration party passed through the area on the way to Klamath Marsh. Later, the railroad headed north through La Pine.

Depending on how big of a hurry you are in, you may want to take Burgess Road west of La Pine to the Cascade Lakes National Scenic Byway. You can purchase your fishing license (in season) along the way, bait your hook and go after some of those fish everyone is talking about. Or just continue on down Highway 97 to the granddaddy of them all, Crater Lake – but notice the "No Fishing" sign. You may be making snowballs or huffing and puffing back up from the bottom of the 600-foot trail that drops down to the water's edge.

Highway 97 takes you all the way to Weed, California, where you will have a spectacular view of Mount Shasta – breathtaking at sunrise. Don't forget, whatever stops you didn't have time for on your way south you can plan to make on your way north. And, thank you, once again, to the pioneers who made this possible. Happy trails to you!

We part more easily with what we possess
than with the expectation of what we wish for:
and the reason of it is,
that what we expect is always greater that what we enjoy.

William Shakespeare (1564-1616)

27

WALK THE OREGON TRAIL NEAR BAKER CITY

Stand at the top of Flagstaff Hill outside Baker City, look down into the valley through the wall of windows at the National Historic Oregon Trail Interpretive Center, and you can see the ruts made by the wheels of the pioneers' wagons.

Better still, traverse down the paved trail and walk in the ruts made by the wagons' wheels to be able to say you did it. The walk back can be a bit challenging but well worth the effort.

In 1803, President Thomas Jefferson organized a secret mission to send the first exploration party overland to the Pacific. Congress approved the trip that would take Lewis and Clark beyond the United States – onto British soil. May of 1804, they started up the Missouri River. December fifth, 1805, they reached the Pacific. They returned from their successful journey to Washington, D.C., with maps, important information, and stories of the difficulties they encountered. No pioneer would ever follow in their footsteps.

The second major westward expedition was funded by the world's richest man, John Jacob Astor, and led by Wilson Price Hunt. His overland pioneer wagon train went through Baker Valley, then known as The Lone Tree Valley, in 1811. Hunt made the first crossing of the Blue Mountains to the Columbia River, establishing a passage for the western part of the Oregon Trail, becoming the major travel route to the West. Hunt arrived in Astoria in 1812.

From 1812 through 1869, more than 250,000 Americans took the Oregon Trail to the West, starting in Independence, Missouri. They crossed the Farewell Bend on the Snake River and conquered the treacherous Burnt River Canyon that led them across Virtue Flat to Flagstaff Hill and into Powder River Valley. By 1890 the population of Baker City was 6,663.

The Oregon Trail Advisory Council was formed in 1984 by executive order of Governor Victor Atiyeh. The Council was responsible for evaluating the condition of the Oregon Trail and reporting to the Governor. In 1990, Governor Barbara Roberts supported the founding of the Oregon Trail Coordinating Council as an independent nonprofit corporation to plan activities for the 1993 sesquicentennial celebration. Planning began for the development of interpretive centers in Baker City, on the Umatilla Indian Reservation near Pendleton, in The Dalles, and in Oregon City.

The National Historic Oregon Trail Interpretive Center on Flagstaff Hill near Baker City opened to record attendance in May, 1992. In 1993 Oregon Legislature provided additional funding for completion of the other three interpretive centers. Funding came from the Oregon Lottery, matching grant programs, and the sale of commemorative license plates.

According to their mission statement: "The National Historic Oregon Trail Interpretive Center at Flagstaff Hill portrays and interprets the Oregon Trail experience and its related themes, while preserving and protecting its historic, cultural heritage, natural, and visual features. The Center serves as a focal point for the cultural heritage traveler, contributes a viable tourism industry for the area, and is committed to maintaining strong community partnerships."

Baker City invites travelers to experience an important part of Oregon's history. An added treat for me was eating at the Geiser Grand Hotel, whose forerunner was the Hotel Warshauer, constructed in 1889. The Warshauer was billed as the most elegant structure between Portland and Denver.

The Center is located about five miles east of Baker City, off I-84, on exit 302 toward Hell's Canyon. The Center is open 9 a.m. to 6 p.m. daily from November 1 through March 31 and from 9 a.m. to 4 p.m. from April 1 to October 31. The Center is closed on major holidays. The Interpretive Center is operated by the Bureau of Land Management and is a federal fee site. Admission for adults is $5 and Children under 15 are free. Federal passes are accepted. For additional information about the Center, contact www.oregontrail.blm.gov, or call 541-523-1843.

We cannot impose our wills on nature
unless we first ascertain what her will is.
Working without regard to law brings nothing but failure;
working with law enables us to do what seemed at first impossible.

Ralph Tyler Flewelling, philosopher

28

MINGLE AMONG THE FOSSILS AT JOHN DAY

If you want to see something really, really old, then plan a visit to the John Day Fossil Beds National Monument.

Historians and paleontologists report a well-preserved, world-renowned fossil record of plants and animals spanning more than 40 of the 65 million years of the Cenozoic Era (the "Age of Mammals and Flowering plants") within the heavily eroded volcanic deposits of the scenic John Day River basin.

Prior to the Fossil Beds designation as a National Monument in 1975, Oregon State Parks officials worked since 1935 to bring 14,000 acres of three State Park Units near Sheep Rock into one of Oregon's most spectacular scenic drives, and stops.

The Visitor Center, located in the Sheep Rock Unit, is 240 miles from Portland, and 122 miles from Bend. The driving distance from the Sheep Rock Unit to the Painted Hills Unit is 45 miles along Highway 26 to Mitchell. From the Painted Hills Unit to Clarno Unit is 75 miles off Highway 218. To complete the loop from Clarno Unit back to Sheep Rock is another 81 miles to get to Highway 19 west of Daysville.

Sheep Rock towers 1,000 feet above the John Day River. The pink and green layers of rock date back approximately 25 to 28 million years, when the three-toed horses and rhinos roamed the land. In addition to the Thomas Condon Paleontology Center and the Cant Ranch Historical Museum, there are several hiking trails, picnic area and wayside exhibits on this Unit.

The yellow, burnished gold, copper, black and reds of the Painted Hills' 3,132 scenic acres are best seen in the late afternoon as the sun sets and the hills catch light and shadows. Wildflower season peaks from late April to early May.

The 1,969 acre Clarno Unit is located 18 miles west of the town of Fossil, and features hiking trails, exhibits and picnic area. The Palisades, formed 44 million years ago by a series of volcanic mudflows called lahars, are the most prominent Clarno landforms. This was the home of tiny four-toed horses, and meat-eating creodonts.

Sites to check weather, museum openings, and campgrounds are www.nps.gov and http://johndayfossilbeds.areaparks.com/campgrounds.

Thirty days hath September,
April, June, and November:
All the rest have thirty-one,
Excepting February alone,
And that has twenty-eight days clear
And twenty-nine in each leap year.

Anonymous

29

PICNIC AT FORT ROCK, OREGON OUTBACK

Turn north at the Fort Rock – Christmas Valley sign off Oregon 31.

A fortress-like volcanic shell from which the homestead town of Fort Rock takes its name is nearly one-third of a mile across, and at its highest point towers 325 feet above the plain on which it stands.

In 1938, University of Oregon professor L.S. Cressman, supervised excavations at Fort Rock Cave, about half a mile west of the crater, and uncovered weapons, tools and dozens of sandals, determined to have been buried at least 7,500 year, below a layer of volcanic ash from Mt. Mazama.

Around 1873, early settler William Sullivan is said to have named the jagged monolith rising out of Oregon's high desert.

There is day parking and a picnic area with facilities at the trailhead for the Fort Rock State Natural Area. Guided tours of Fort Rock Cave leave from there and arrangements are made by calling La Pine State Park.

Before you come to Fort Rock road, you will want to stop at Fort Rock Valley Historical Homestead Museum to your right.

Eight charter members opened the Homestead Village with two buildings in 1988. Since then, several more buildings have been brought from surrounding homestead sites, and more members of the Historical Society maintain the grounds. The museum and village is open to the public from Memorial Day weekend until the weekend after Labor Day, on Friday, Saturday and Sunday from 9:00 am to dusk.

Be sure to visit these furnished 1870s buildings – pride and joy of the homesteaders: St. Rose's Church, Mekenmair Cabin, Webster Cabin, Dr. Thom's Office, Bodenhiemer House, Belletable House, Sunset School, The Land Office, and the Fred Stratton House.

St. Rose's Catholic Church, the only designated homestead church building in the whole valley, was moved from a corner of the Godon ranch and saved from vandalism by the Fort Rock Historical Society. The Sunset School, only one of 20 valley schools remaining, was moved from half way between Derrick and Stingley ranches.

On a wall, as you enter the schoolhouse, you will want to read the plaque with the "1872 Rules for Teachers." No mention of merit pay.

In addition to filling, lighting and cleaning lamps, teachers were expected to bring a bucket of water and a scuttle of coal for each session. Men teachers were given one evening a week for courting purposes, whereas women teachers who married were dismissed. Teachers performing their duties faultlessly for five years were given a 25-cent per week increase in pay. In addition, a teacher was expected to "lay aside from each day pay a goodly sum of his earnings for his benefit during his declining years so that he will not become a burden on society."

And, 12 miles up the road northeast from the Homestead Village through Christmas Valley you can take a two-mile stroll or hike through the 70 foot deep Crack in the Ground. Watch for signs.

The Crack in the Ground fissure was formed about 1,100 years ago when flowing lava cooled. There is an established trail the length of the fissure's bottom. On a hot day it is 20 degrees cooler on the lower trail than where you park your car. Because this fissure is located in an arid region it has not filled with soil and rock from erosion and sedimentation. It exists today much as when it occurred.

If you are ready for more adventure you can look for the Hole in the Ground. We did, but found it less than spectacular after the Crack in the Ground, Fort Rock and the Homestead Village. So much to see on Oregon's Scenic Outback drive.

Go tell it on the mountain – spiritual
Hear, O mountain, the plea of the Lord – scripture
Faith to move mountains – saying

The shadows now so long do grow.
That brambles like tall cedars show,
Molehills seem mountains, and the ant
Appears a monstrous elephant.

Charles Cotton (1630-1687)

30

STEENS MOUNTAIN NATIONAL BACK COUNTRY BYWAY

Modern civilization seems to have a fixation with mountains since Moses went up to Mt. Sinai and came down with the Ten Commandments. Some adventurers want to *climb every mountain* – as in *The Sound of Music* – and others simply enjoy the view.

In Central Oregon there are mountains to ski, climb or admire from a distance. I lived in the Portland area from more than 30 years and hiked a multitude of trails around Mt. Hood, Mt. Rainier, Mt Adams and Mt. St. Helens. I've skied Bachelor and Hood. And, can now say I have been on the 52-mile Steens Mountain Loop road.

I once had a friend who timed his travels, coast to coast, to photograph the first blooms of the wildflowers in the spring or the last color of nature in autumn.

Spring comes late in the higher elevations of Steens Mountain in southeast Oregon, attracting botanists, artists and photographers from late June, when the gravel road to the top opens, until the snow flies at the end of summer.

Although the reputation and the legends of the Steens had not escaped me during the more than 40 years I lived in Oregon, the opportunities to visit the Steens had.

Friends in Bend, Oregon go to the Steens every year to check out the wildflowers and absorb the mystery and the magic of the mountain. In mid-July we met up with them at the Brothers rest stop on Hwy. 20 outside Bend. We then caravanned in our motor homes to Hwy. 205 outside Burns. We drove 60 miles south to Frenchglen, not far from the Nevada border, where we picked up the gravel road to the BLM Page Springs Campground Area.

There's no electric or water hookups at the campground, but the RV spaces are huge and the setting is peaceful and relaxing along the Blitzen River. There are four campgrounds along the backcountry byway. We stayed two nights, having divided the main meal planning and preparation and using plenty of mosquito repellent.

The next morning our friends introduced us to Steens Mountain. According to the literature there is only one mountain, no foothills. You don't realize you are above the 9,000 ft. level until you take a short trail down to the Wildhorse Lake outlook and then back up again.

We stopped at all the spectacular viewpoints: Kiger Gorge, East Rim, Big Indian Gorge, Little Blitzen Gorge, and Wildhorse Lake outlook. While sitting on a rock at the edge of the Kiger Gorge, I listened to the history of the mountain and its people in the silence and from the wind. Patches of snow on the higher curves of the bowl-shaped ravine were contrasted with the deep green along the river bed far below.

Referred to as "Nature's Bulldozer" the four immense V-shaped gorges on Steens Mountain were formed by glaciers digging trenches during the Ice Age. The east edge of the Steens was raised up from underground pressure along a fault line, creating a 30-milelong fault-block mountain with a mile-high east face above the Alvord Desert.

As air heats up in the Alvord Basin and rises on the east face of the Steens you can see golden eagles and other raptors riding the wind currents along the rim of the Kiger Gorge. An estimated

300 wild horses, numerous antelope and other smaller animals make their home at various locations on the Steens.

Earliest inhabitants, native Americans, camped at the foot of the mountain and moved further up the mountain as the snow melted in the spring and the green grass was exposed for grazing. Later, in the mid-1800s ranchers and goat herders moved on to the mountain slopes.

The rivers were named "Donner und Blitzen," German for thunder and lightening, by Captain George B. Curry in 1864 when he crossed in a thunderstorm in pursuit of Indians.

In 1872, when Pete French saw the green grass and constant water supply of the Blitzen Valley he built the largest single cattle ranch in the United States – in just 28 years. The former P-Ranch is one mile east of Frenchglen.

In the early 1900s, the Riddle brothers, Walter and Fred, settled in the Little Blitzen Valley, where they built a ranch and made their living for more than 40 years. The Bureau of Land Management since has purchased the ranch for its historical value.

Now, the Steens Mountain Cooperative Management and Protection Area represent 496,136 acres of private and public land.

Meditation walk taking in the wonder of it all.

When we gradually worked our way up the mountain in mid-July, stopping at lakes, valleys and meadows, some of the wildflowers at the lower levels had already bloomed and died, although plenty of others were still in their glory. We stopped to talk with an artist from Sisters, Oregon who brought her water color class into the meadow where they were capturing the colorful scenery on canvas with brushes and paint.

After reaching the top of the mountain and viewing the gorges and other outlooks, travelers have the option of returning on the same, good road, or venturing down the rough road on the south side of the mountain. The south road is not recommended for motor homes, trailers or vehicles, and cars with low clearance.

Although the south road is rocky, steep, and narrow in places, we viewed beautiful valleys and landscape, stopped at our friends favorite meditation point, and had the entire 52-mile loop experience. I am grateful to have seen this special place that brings so many here each summer. Did the mountain speak to me? Perhaps.

What you need to know

- For road conditions and other Steens Mountain information, go to: www.harneycounty.com/SteensMtn.htm. The entire loop is usually open from July 1 to October 31, depending on snow conditions. For information on public camping facilities and dates, or weather call BLM: 541-573-4400.
- There are four BLM fee campgrounds with drinking water and vault toilets located at Page Springs, Fish Lake, Jackman Park, and South Steens. There is a private campground, gas, phone, and store at Frenchglen.
- The Frenchglen Historic Hotel has eight family-style rooms with shared bath. Breakfast, lunch and dinner are made to order. Reservations recommended. On our way out of the Steens area we had breakfast of French toast, bacon, and coffee from the big farmhouse coffee pot. The Hotel, established in

1916, is open from March 15 to November 15. For information call 541-493-2825.

- Other area lodging includes Steens Mountain Resort: 541-493-2415. Drover's Inn: 541-493-2204. Hotel Diamond: 541-493-1898. McCoy Creek Inn: 541-493-2131.

Our object in traveling should be,
not to gratify curiosity,
and seek mere temporary amusement,
but to learn, and to venerate,
to improve the understanding and the heart.

William Gresley

31

YOSEMITE – MILLIONS OF YEARS IN THE MAKING

Millions of years ago, the California's Sierra Nevada Mountains and valleys were formed by a gradual series of earth upheavals. As the mountains rose, the torrential waters of the Merced River carved the narrow Merced Canyon. Then, massive glaciers ground down and polished rock formations in the Yosemite Valley, and made way for some of the worlds most spectacular waterfalls.

Many roads lead to Yosemite, most are open all year. Some are more difficult than others depending on how large a rig you drive and how much you have in tow. On the map 140 looks like a less desirable choice than 120, but 120 is long, curvy and difficult. Many RV adventurers park their big rigs in Mariposa, Midpines, Briceburg or El Portal, and drive their cars in the rest of the way for day trips. Coming from the west on 120 there are RV sites at Big Oak Flat, Buck Meadows and Harden Flat. The road from the east on 120 is closed in winter. For road conditions call 209-372-0200, or contact www.nps.gov/yose.

There are 13 campgrounds inside the park. During peak season there is a seven-day limit in the North Pines, Upper Pines, Lower Pines and Camp 4 campgrounds in Yosemite Valley. There are no hookups. Regulations and reservation information for Yosemite and 387 other national parks and 440 campgrounds can be found on www.nps.gov/yose/trip/camping.htm and www.reservations.nps.gov.

Considering the millions of years achieving the miracle of Yosemite, our two full days and two full nights only whet the adventurer's appetite.

Day 1 – We entered Yosemite Park from the south on highway 41, after spending the previous night at an RV camp in Oakhurst, and stopping at the must-see Pioneer Yosemite History Center. We called ahead for reservations and stayed in the Upper Pines Campground, half price with Golden Age Passport.

Car and RV parking is limited in the valley, so we walked or took the shuttle bus while there. Free shuttles run every 10 to 15 minutes during peak season. First we made the loop, then bought tickets for the National Park Service guided tram tour. Since we drove in from the south entrance we already had some of Yosemite's marvelous landmarks.

El Capitan, a massive, granite monolith that standing 3,593 feet from the base to the summit, claims to be the largest granite monolith in the world. Rock climbers come from all over the world for this one.

We saw Half Dome from our RV space, and observed changes in color on the gigantic rock from early morning to late afternoon. This 8,842 monument is only 87 million years young, and the missing half of the dome is said to have sheered off during its ancient cooling phase. We heard some sheering, as rocks rumbled down the cliff.

As is true of most of our national parks, the native inhabitants of this continent discovered these beautiful places long before the Europeans arrived. The Yosemite Valley was inhabited more than 6,000 years ago, and the Southern Sierra Miwok Indians lived in the valley when the Euro-Americans arrived in the mid-19th century.

The 1848, discovery of gold in California brought thousands of prospectors to the Yosemite area. Few non-Indians knew of the existence of the Valley prior to the discovery of gold in the Sierra foothills. By 1851, the continued theft of Indian lands and murder of native people resulted in the Mariposa Indian War. The state-sanctioned Mariposa Battalion engaged to subdue the Indian uprising were the first non-Indians to record entry into the Valley. Yosemite's reputation grew and tourists began to arrive.

In the middle of the Civil War a group of influential Californians persuaded Congress and President Abraham Lincoln to grant Yosemite Valley and the Mariposa Grove to the state of California as its first public preserve. This was accomplished when Abraham Lincoln signed the Yosemite Grant on June 30, 1864.

The grant, considered to be the foundation upon which national parks were later established, did not protect the vast wilderness surrounding the Valley and sequoia grove.

Conservationist John Muir first visited the Valley in 1868. By 1872, Muir, and Robert Underwood Johnson, editor of *Century Magazine,* had joined forces in lobbying to preserve the entire area. Johnson used his contacts with important private citizens and politicians on the east coast, and Muir spoke and wrote eloquently of the need for the legislation to set aside more than 1,500 square miles of "reserved forest lands" that surrounded, but did not include, Yosemite Valley and the Mariposa Grove of Giant Sequoias. The U.S. Congress passed legislation on October 1, 1890, paving the way for the country's second national park. Yellowstone National Park was established in 1872.

To complete the Yosemite National Park picture, in 1906, at the urging of John Muir and railroad magnate Edward H. Harriman, President Theodore Roosevelt had Yosemite Valley and Mariposa Grove ceded from the state of California's control and included as part of the Yosemite National Park.

Day 2 – In the morning we watched a group of school children heading for a hike and followed them to the trailhead to Vernal and Nevada falls. That is one relatively short but strenuous uphill walk, and we went as far as the Vernal Fall footbridge. We hear from younger hikers that the seven mile round-trip trail to the top of Nevada Fall is challenging and, for them, worth the effort.

Ansel Adams Gallery – Be sure to visit the Ansel Adams Gallery. His name and marvelous black and white photography are forever connected with Yosemite's waterfalls, rivers, valleys, and rock formations – especially El Capitan.

Yosemite is still a photographer's dream. Most of us, however, now use color film, video or digital cameras. Yet the mystic beauty captured by Adams' black and white photography demands our attention – and we see the wonders of nature as he saw them.

Adams died in 1984 at the age of 82, but his legacy lives on at the gallery in the heart of the Yosemite Valley, next to the Visitor Center, Museum, and Park Service Headquarters.

For an overall orientation see the film *Spirit of Yosemite* in the Valley Visitor Center Theater. During your visit to the Museum you can listen to Julia Parker, Coastal Miwok Indian, tell traditional and historical stories, while she weaves her popular baskets; then tour a representation of a Miwok Indian village.

For lunch, we enjoyed Shrimp Pasta and Chinese Chicken Salad in the historic and amazing Ahwahnee dining room, with its 34-foot-tall trestle-beamed ceiling, floor-to-ceiling windows and many twinkling chandeliers. Dinnertime requires "proper attire," and the cost is considerably more.

We came to Yosemite Valley to see its numerous waterfalls and watch with amazement as the sunlight and shadows create a constantly changing landscape. Don't miss what the Ahwahneechee called Bridalveil Fall, "Spirit of the Puffing Wind," and stand back from the 620-foot drop or bring an umbrella for protection.

Yosemite Falls is actually two waterfalls, dropping a combined total of 2,425 feet, to become the tallest waterfall in North America – about twice the height of the Empire State Building. It's an easy walk from the shuttle to the lower fall. Walk through the spray, but keep your camera dry for a better view, later.

Other wondrous sights include: Mirror Lake, Valley View Turnout, Tunnel View, Wawona, Mariposa Grove of Giant Sequoias, Glacier Point Road, Badger Pass, Hetch Hetchy, Tioga Road and

High County, Tuolummne Meadows, and more – time and weather permitting.

Millions of years in the making – Yosemite's natural and cultural treasure needs to be preserved for future generations of nature lovers, campers, hikers, artists and photographers while providing for the enjoyment of millions of visitors annually.

Mr. Marshall called me to come to him.
I went and found him examining the bed rock.
He said, 'This is a curious rock.
I am afraid that it will give us trouble,'
and as he probed it a little further, he said,
'I believe that it contains minerals of some kind,
and I believe that there is gold in these hills.

Recollection (1848) by James Brown

32

DISCOVER CALIFORNIA'S GOLD RUSH TOWNS

Heading north to Oregon, after wintering in Mexico, we picked up California Highway 49 in Mariposa. At that juncture, we visited the Mariposa Museum and Historic Center, with it representation of the life and times of the first inhabitants, through the Indian and Spanish periods, to the Gold Rush era.

From the Mariposa Museum we were directed to the California State Mining and Mineral Museum, located on the County Fairgrounds two miles south of town. There, we saw California's largest existing Gold Rush specimen of crystallized gold – the Fricot Nugget weighs almost 13 pounds. Also on display was a five-foot-tall working model of the stamp mill gold processing system, as well as a 25-inch long copper sheet, just as it was found.

The 1848 discovery of gold in California brought people and industrialization to the lush wilderness, farmlands, mountains and rivers that might not have seen that kind of growth for two more generations – and the state has grown by leaps and bounds ever since.

Native Nisenan and foothill Miwok people who had inhabited the area for thousands of years in villages along streams and tributaries of the American River were diminished by diseases introduced by newcomers in the 1820s and 1830s. Some of the remaining natives worked for settlers, and later were caught up in the gold mining, most were dispersed to more remote areas of the Gold Country.

Fortunately, preserved historic landmarks, renovated old towns and nature's wonders along the Highway 49 "Gold Rush Trail" continue to display their welcome mats to car and RV travelers headed from north to south in autumn, and from south to north in spring, or anytime in between. On our trip in early May, we encountered off-and-on rain – an outstanding display of purple and white wild flowers as well as California's yellow poppies – all the way up Highway 49.

Summer months could prove to be the ideal time to travel this route.

This scenic highway and its byways provide opportunities for enjoyment for antique shoppers, historical buffs, those who appreciate the great outdoors, and those who appreciate good food and comfortable lodging, or RV parks. You can take a day, a week or longer – depending on how many stops you want to make, how many "Loops" you want to take, how much of the history and scenery you want to experience.

According to *California's Gold Country Visitor Guide* "as more and more miners arrived, the gold fields expanded, first to tributaries of the American River, then to other rivers to the north and south. Eventually the boundaries of the 'Mother Lode' were established as a 120-mile strip running from just northeast of Coloma on the north to Mariposa on the south."

Before leaving Mariposa we picked up a handful of Gold Country maps and brochures. Our first stop was Jamestown – bypassing the Hornitos-Snelling-La Grange side loop and the Jacksonville Road side trip.

We walked the streets of Jamestown with its charming old buildings and hanging baskets of flowers. Also hanging outside the Gold Prospecting Store was an effigy of a would-be minor who probably "jumped a claim." The town, named after its founder Colonel George James, is near the site where gold was first discovered in Tuolumne County by James Woods in 1848.

Farther up the road, we pulled into the 49er RV Ranch with our Roadtrek RV for a night. The 49er RV Ranch advertises "Old Ranch Hospitality Since 1852,"and they are located a few miles from the Columbia State Historic Park "where the gold rush lives." The park is open year round with interactive attractions for young and old, and special events throughout the year. Their claim is "the best-preserved gold-rush town in all of California's Mother Lode."

Welcome signs are out at San Andreas, Mokelumne Hill, Jackson, Sutter Creek, Amador City, Drytown, Plymouth, Diamond Springs, and Placerville – all the way to the Marshall Gold Discovery State Historic Park at Coloma, the centerpiece for the "Golden State's" Highway 49. Here is where it all began, when James Marshall shared his discovery with workers at the sawmill construction site.

In 1845, John Sutter, founder of Sutter's Fort, hired Marshall, who had come to the Mexican possession of California from Missouri by way of Oregon. In exchange for his carpentry skills, Sutter provided him with land and cattle. Later, Marshall volunteered and served in the Mexican—American war during the Bear Flag Revolt.

After leaving his battalion Marshall returned to his ranch to discover his cattle gone, and without income he lost his land. He soon entered into a partnership with Capt. John Sutter to oversee construction and operation of his sawmill. In return, Marshall would receive a portion of the lumber. The sawmill would produce lumber needed for Sutter's gristmill.

A year after starting work on the project, the mill was ready for testing. When they opened the gates, the tailrace, which carried water away from the mill, was too shallow. Water backed up and prevented the wheel from turning. Indian laborers loosened the rock to deepen the tailrace, and water was released to wash away the soil and debris.

On the morning of January 24, 1848, Marshall scooped up some tiny flecks of gold in the tailrace, tested the metal in the presence of some of his workers, and then rode to Sutter's Fort to share the news. The gold rush was on – and the rest is history.

At Marshall Gold Discovery State Historical Park you can experience history. Visit the museum, the Wah Hop Store, the

Man Lee Mining Exhibit, a Miner's Cabin with all the tools and a Mormon Cabin set up for daily comfort, the Waller House, Bell's Store Ruins, a Blacksmith Shop, and other replicas of the old town. More importantly – walk the mill site trails along the South Fork American River; stand at the Sawmill Replica – and imagine what it was like to see gold come out of the river and out of the ground, and to gain or lose a fortune.

History: There's gold in these hills

Many lengthy reports of the gold rush years are available on www.sfmuseum.org, allowing visitors to the Gold Rush area to become well informed before hitting that trail – or after, as their interest peaks.

One of the reports titled "The Discovery of Gold in California" by Gen. John A. Sutter appeared in *Hutchings' California Magazine*, November 1857. Sutter tells of the rise and fall of his personal empire. (Sutter is referred to as a Capt. in other reports. So he will be here.) Capt. Sutter was the founder of "New Helvetia. Later named Sacramento – where he held vast agricultural acreage in the Sacramento Valley. He needed a sawmill to get lumber to finish his large flouring mill and other buildings at Brighton.

Another report titled "California Gold: an authentic history of the first find with the names of those interested in the discovery" was written by James Brown of Salt Lake City, Utah on January 24, 1894,

According to Brown, in August of 1847, at the end of the Mexican-American war over the California territory, he was among the 150-member detachment of the Mormon Battalion on its way back to Utah.

While camped on the American Fork River about two miles from Sutter's Fort, 100 of the men from the battalion struck a deal with James Marshall to stay behind and provide skilled labor for the building of a sawmill for Sutter. Marshall promised to pay the carpenters, blacksmiths, wheelwrights, millwrights, farmers and common laborers at the end of the project. Part of the pay would be in the form of horses, cattle, and supplies for crossing the plains to Utah.

Some of the Mormon men were employed to work on the gristmill, some took contracts on the mill race of that mill, others – including James Brown were hired to follow Marshall to the location for the saw mill – at the bend in the American River.

On January 24, 1848, Brown reports that "Mr. Marshall called me to come to him. I went, and found him examining the bed rock. He said, 'This is a curious rock, I am afraid that it will give us trouble,' and as he probed it a little further, he said, 'I believe that it contains minerals of some kind, and I believe that there is gold in these hills.'"

When Marshall was certain he'd found gold he operated with great secrecy; taking samples to Capt. Sutter, who proceeded having a heavy ring made for himself – engraved with his family crest on the outside and "The first gold, discovered in January 1848" on the inside.

As word spread, men came by ship from Hawaii and around Cape Horn from the east coast. They came down from the Oregon Territory, up from Mexico, from all reaches of the United States, and as far away as China. Historians report that by winter of 1848, when the rains stopped the mining, there were more than 5,000 men in the "diggings."

James Brown recalled that when men from the sawmill camp first heard about the discovery they started taking day trips up and down the river on the pretense of duck hunting or some other matter, and came back with gold wrapped in their handkerchiefs. Brown recounts how the secret gradually seeped out.

"And somehow or other the bag came untied and our old cat and all the kittens ran out, and to the camps they went, until everybody heard them. But, like all great truths, people were slow to believe the story."

James Brown contends that the Mormon laborers should be given some credit for gold discovery. Mormon Island is named for those who left the sawmill and came back from Utah to dig or pan for gold.

"It is confirmed in my mind that had it not been for this opportunity, the sawmill at least, would not have been built, nor the discovery of gold been made at that time. The State of California would have waited indefinitely to have been developed and to be christened the 'Golden State,' and the entrance to San Francisco Bay might never have received the title of the 'Golden Gate.'"

Before leaving for the Utah Territory, Brown said he "worked 100 days for the firm, and never received one farthing for it." The reason being, Capt. Sutter was ruined financially by the gold rush. But, Brown doesn't blame Sutter "...their business affairs were undermined, and there was a general collapse of every industry and business. The cry was 'gold! gold! more gold! Away for the gold fields!' Every enterprise was sacrificed at the sight of gold."

"What a great misfortune was this sudden gold discovery for me!" said Capt. Sutter. "It has just broken up and ruined my hard, restless, and industrious labors." According to him, when the gold fever struck, every man who could packed-up and set out for the gold fields, leaving Sutter without laborers to finish his mills and other enterprises.

Where to go for information

Highway 49 passes through nine of California's most beautiful counties. Information about activities and points of interest can be gathered from the following state and county sites:

Amador County Chamber of Commerce & Visitors Bureau
www.amadorcountychamber.com

Calaveras Visitors Bureau
www.visitcalaveral.org

El Dorado County Chamber of Commerce
www.eldoradocounty.org or www.visit-eldorado.com

Grass Valley/Nevada County Chamber of Commerce
www.gvnchamber.org

Placer County Visitors Council and California Welcome Center
www.visitplacer.com

Tuolumne County Visitors Bureau
www.TheGreatUnfenced.com

California State Parks
www.parks.ca.gov

Gold Country Visitors Association
www.calgold.org

A land of surprises
around each colorful corner
where everyone's imagination runs free.

LEGO Company promo
LEGOLAND California

33

FAMILY FUN AT LEGOLAND CALIFORNIA

Do you remember those colorful, little plastic interlocking blocks that our kids used play with and build all sorts of houses, vehicles, bridges and skyscrapers? Sometimes the blocks didn't all get back in the box or bag and we stepped on them while passing through the living room in our bare feet. Ouch!

LEGOS initially were made of wood, and they are slightly older than I am. Ole Kirk Christiansen started making wooden toys in his Billund, Denmark workshop in 1932. Two years later, he named his toys and workshop LEGO, from the Danish words "leg godt," meaning "play well." Also, the word LEGO in Latin means "I put together."

Our youngsters are often shocked to know we existed before "plastic." Oh, how plastic changed our world, and our toys. The forerunner to the LEGO brick was introduced in 1949, under the name "Automatic Binding Bricks." Then, the plastics injection-molding machine began producing the marvelous little and bigger, interlocking building bricks that we've all enjoyed so much.

In March of 1999, LEGO Company opened its fourth LEGOLAND theme park on 128-acres, about 12 miles north of San Diego, off of the I-5 in Carlsbad. It is described in their promotional literature as "a land of surprises around each colorful corner where everyone's imagination runs free.

"Discover kid-powered rides, cool building challenges, a unique mix of interactive attractions, exhilarating roller coasters, shows that pull the audience into the action, astonishingly accurate and whimsical LEGO brick models and so much more."

The first LEGOLAND in Billund, Denmark began as an outdoor garden exhibit – and it grew and it grew. All of buildings, landscapes and vehicles were constructed with standard LEGO bricks. The nine-acre park opened June 1968, and saw 625,000 happy visitors that first year. LEGOLAND Windsor opened outside London in 1996, and LEGOLAND Deutschland in Germany opened 2002.

Just imagine building an entire LEGO theme park on your living room floor, with zoo animals, people, robots, boats, and vehicles of all kinds – some with moving parts – and miniature cities and structures. Then magnify everything bigger-than-life. That's why kids and adults are blown away by the similarities, and imaginative difference with what they have been building with their own hands. And, it's a great opportunity for adults to become kids again.

Our adult children in Anchorage, Alaska had previously visited LEGOLAND California, with our three grandchildren – and couldn't stop talking about it. They suggested we drive up from our winter home in San Felipe, Baja Norte, Mexico and meet them in San Diego during the kids' Spring Break. We are always delighted when we have family visit us, or we can come together with some or all of them anywhere, any time in the states.

We drove the Roadtrek 190 RV up to San Diego. My daughter Sheila and her husband Dee (my husband's son) flew into San Diego with our three grandchildren, from toddler to teenager. My husband's daughter Becky drove down from Port Hadlock, Washington, with her family. My daughter Teresa and her family had been at Disneyland (from Portland, Oregon) and drove down to LEGOLAND.

We were among the first in line to enter the LEGOLAND parking lot. We went all the way to the end, nearest the gate. We parked our RV and blocked off three spaces next to ours with orange cones I borrowed from where they were blocking an exit.

We were in touch with the others by cell phone, so they knew where to find us, and they started rolling in right on schedule. They were mighty grateful we had our refrigerator with sodas and sandwiches – as well as a handy-dandy lavatory.

There were eight adults, two teenagers, three pre-teens and two toddlers. In all that represented nearly half our family.

All rides in the park are included in the price of admission. The two teenagers took off on their own for the Driving School and the LEGO Technic Coaster. The three younger children headed for Sky Patrol in Fun Town, and Spellbreaker and The Dragon in Castle Hill. Then, there was Sky Cruiser at the Ridge and Aquazone Wave Racers in the Imagination Zone.

The rest of us hung around with the toddlers in Playtown, a scaled-down village with its rides and activities, and plenty of hands-and feet-on play experiences. We helped them build "things," rode on the coaster, and ate popcorn and other treats. Strollers were provided, but the toddlers preferred to be up and running, or walking, most of the time.

We were amazed at how much fun an adult can have in a kid's theme park. And the Miniland attraction with its detailed, animated depiction of New York City, Washington, DC, Colonial America and the California coast captured our attention.

I enjoyed a boat ride with my two toddler grandsons down Fairy Tale Brook, and shared their excitement watching the three pigs pop out from their houses of straw, sticks and brick. Best of all we spent quality time with adult children and grandchildren – doing something they all thoroughly enjoyed.

We were among the first to enter the park and among the last to leave. We had plenty of time to visit with family members, young and older. Someone in each group had a walkie-talkie so that we could all come back together within some reasonable time frames. And when the kids ran out of snack funds they could call up for more. It was a great place for a reunion. For more information, go to www.lego.com.

America's first native breed,
the Morgan is noted for stamina, dependability and intelligence.
The Morgan Horse Ranch is the only operational horse breeding ranch
in our National Park system.
The horses are trained for use as ranger patrol mounts
in our Western National Parks.

Sign posted at Point Reyes, CA

34

POINT REYES, CA – BASE CAMP TO SIX AMAZING PARKS

Point Reyes Station is one of those "feel good" small towns with a health food grocery store, art galleries and restaurants. You are just passing through when you decide to stop for coffee and pastries at the bakery, where you sit on a bench out front and watch the locals and visitors come and go.

If you come from the south on California Coast Highway One, you are in for some of Marin County's most spectacular scenery. Because we travel in a Road trek 190 RV we were able to maneuver the twists and turns of Highway One from the Golden Gate Bridge to Olema – not recommended for vehicles over 35 feet. Larger RVs take Highway 101 to either San Rafael or Petaluma exit.

Whether you're coming from the north or the south, Olema or Point Reyes Station serve as base camp to the 65,000 acre Point Reyes National Seashore, with its historic lighthouse. While staying in the area you are close to five other wonder parks: Tomales Bay State Park, Samuel P. Taylor State Park, Golden Gate National

Recreation Area, Muir Woods National Monument with its giant redwoods, and Mount Tamalpais State Park.

We stayed at the Olema Ranch Campground in a largely underdeveloped part of West Marin County on SR-1. The campground had 89 RV sites, over 100 tent sites, and located a short distance from the Bear Valley Visitors Center. The visitor's center provides films, exhibits and information about Point Reyes National Seashore.

The Point Reyes Peninsula barely hangs on to the mainland along the San Andreas Fault line. Early explores believed it was an island when they sailed deep into the Tomales Bay from the north. Point Reyes National Seashore lies on a scenic stretch of SR-1 that extends from Leggett to Sausalito.

The Miwoks, a peaceful people, inhabited the land long before Sir Francis Drake, an English adventurer in the service of Queen Elizabeth I, sailed his ship *Golden Hind* off the shore in 1579. History notes that he careened his ship and stayed in the area five weeks to make repairs. Meanwhile the Miwoks supplied them with boiled fish and meal ground from wild roots.

Drake named the area New England, as the high cliffs resembled the Dover coast of the English Channel. Explorers came and went. During a storm on January 6, 1693, Spanish explorer Don Sebastian Vizcaino was battling winds in Drake's Bay. Heading back to sea he sailed past the rocky headlands and gave Point Reyes its name. He called it La Punta de Los Tres Reyes because it was the Feast of the Three Kings.

When settlers of Mexico and California revolted against the Spanish in 1821 they established an Independent Republic of Mexico. By that time there were few of the original Miwok inhabitants to be found. They had been taken from their homeland to labor in the Spanish missions. Today you can visit Kule Loklo, a replica of a Miwok Indian Village.

After the United States conquered California the flatlands of Point Reyes were broken into dozens of dairy ranches. Today, the Pierce Ranch, one of the former dairy ranches has self-guiding trail exhibits.

From the Point Reyes visitors center you may have time, or take time, to hike the 0.7 – Earthquake Trail along the San Andreas Fault or the Woodpecker Nature Trail. You can ride a horse or a bike – or simply see where the road leads. A drive to Drake's Beach, famed for its high, white cliffs will make a great picnic spot. Operational since 1870, the Point Reyes Lighthouse can be reached by descending 300 steps below the observation platform. The return trip is equivalent to walking up the stairs of a 30-story building. You may settle for the observation platform to look seaward for elephant seals, sea lions, Killer Whales or Gray Whales.

Be sure to visit the Morgan Horse Ranch, a short walk up the hill from the visitor center. The National Park Service raises and trains their horses there for use in the park. There are miles of horse trails, and the Park Service patrols. According to the sign at the ranch:

"America's first native breed, the Morgan is noted for stamina, dependability and intelligence." Also noted, "The Morgan Horse Ranch is the only operational horse breeding ranch in our National Park System. The horses here are being trained for use as ranger patrol mounts in our Western National Parks."

Car camping is prohibited inside the park. There are four hike-in campgrounds, and permits are required. Hiking trails of varying lengths are accessible from the trailheads on the road. Pick up your maps at the Visitors Center. For more information, go to www.pointreyes.net. And don't forget to stop for coffee and pastry at Point Reyes Station bakery.

We had a great time!
We liked what we were doin' and we did it with a great amount of flair.
We did it with a propensity towards 'Ready or not, here we come!'
The road had the lonely times, but I kept myself busy.

Buck Owens, country western singer

35

WHEN BAKERSFIELD WAS BUCKERSFIELD

Passing by or through Bakersfield on our way to Mexico each year I asked my husband, "Anything there we want to see?" His answer for seven years had been "No!"

Since he served two tours of duty at Edwards Air Force Base in the Mojave Desert many years ago, I thought he should know. However, much to our surprise, one year we discovered the Buck Owens' Crystal Palace on Buck Owens Drive, off Hwy. 99.

I vaguely remembered the name, associated with the Buckaroos band, the "Buck Owens' Ranch" and "Hee Haw" TV shows, as well as a few Capitol records hits such as "Act Naturally," "Hot Dog," "Love's Gonna Live Here," "My Heart Skips A Beat," and "I've Got A Tiger By The Tail."

On October 27, 2006, less than a year after the passing of Buck Owens on March 25, we were staying at the Best Western Motel and went next door to the Crystal Palace for the early show. When they told us Buddy Alan Owens was the featured performer it still hadn't registered with me that we were in for a special treat, seeing and hearing the son of the "man himself," and the Buckaroos "themselves."

The two-story tiered and balconied interior of the Crystal Palace is a restaurant, concert stage, dance hall, and museum. In response to my questions Terry Christoffersen, general manager said:

"Buck had the Crystal Palace built so he could share his experiences and memorabilia from around the world with his fans. He also wanted a place where he could comfortably perform his music without having to travel like he had done in his younger days. We opened on October 23, 1996 and haven't slowed down yet."

Inside the entrance of the Crystal Palace visitors may view and pose for photos with one or more of the 10 larger-than-life statues of country stars Buck Owens considered to be legends of country music – Johnny Cash, Hank Williams Sr., Willie Nelson, George Jones, George Strait, Garth Brooks, Merle Haggard, Elvis Presley, Bob Wills, and of course, himself.

According to Christoffersen, Owens had planned on commissioning some female stars to the collection in the future, but he didn't have time to make that happen, and "the Crystal Palace continues to be a world-class entertainment venue, restaurant and tribute to the life of Buck Owens.

We stopped at the Crystal Palace again this year to feast on baby back ribs, listen to some good country music, and dodge the other dancers.

How Bakersfield Became Buckersfield

Alvis Edgar Owens, Jr. was the firstborn child, on August 12, 1929, to sharecropper Alvis and his wife Marcie Owens, on the land they tilled outside Sherman, Texas. When Alvis Jr. was three or four years old he announced that he was renaming himself "Buck" after a mule on the Owens' farm.

Buck's mother played piano and exposed her children to gospel music. Buck said he knew without question "what he *didn't* want." He had a dream of a better life of "not going to bed hungry, or wearing hand-me-down clothes." When he was 16 he teamed up with a 19-year-old guitarist. They became "Buck and Britt" and played on local radio and at honky-tonks, where they passed the hat for pay, before moving west to Phoenix.

Buck married Bonnie Campbell in 1948, and their first son Alan "Buddy" was born to follow in his father's musical footsteps. In 1951, Buck and Bonnie moved with their two sons to Bakersfield, where the oil fields and farmlands had become home for refugees from the Dust Bowl of Texas and Oklahoma. Buck joined a band led by guitarist Dusty Rhodes, and then went with the Orange Blossom Playboys at the Blackboard, Bakersfield's top country music nightclub, until 1958.

Owens played and sang harmony at the LuTal Recording Studio in Bakersfield, and later signed with Capitol for solo recordings. In 1958, Owens moved to Puyallup, Washington to take over 250-watt radio station KAYE, and began his own live TV show over KTNT in Tacoma. By June of 1960 his recordings were hitting the charts and he divested himself of the Washington holdings and returned to Bakersfield, permanently.

For the next several years Buck Owens traveled to gigs around the country in an old Ford, then thousands of miles in an old Chevy camper, and finally a bus with the band, until he quit the road in 1980. He boasted that he never missed a date, playing at clubs from 9 at night until 1 in the morning, without leaving the stage.

In the mid-sixties, Owens branched out with a booking agency and a progression of radio stations, KUZZ-AM, and then KKXX-FM in Bakersfield, then KTUF-AM, and KNIX-FM in Phoenix, all consolidated under Buck Owens Productions.

By 1966, Buck Owens, Merle Haggard, Tommy Collins and Wynn Stewart, each with his own style on Capitol records, defined what was then referred to as the "Bakersfield Sound," reminiscent of the honky-tonk days. Owens finally made a pledge to his fans, "I refuse to be known as anything but a country singer. I am proud to be associated with country music."

Buck Owens and the Buckaroos played Grand Ole Opry, Carnegie Hall and for Lyndon Johnson at the White House, dressed in their rhinestone studded Nudie outfits, and with steel guitars and musical instruments painted red, white and blue.

Owens bought an old movie theater in downtown Bakersfield and opened his own recording studio, and the media started referring to Bakersfield as "Buckersfield." His national exposure, however, came from the "Buck Owens' Ranch" TV show and, "Hee Haw" the CBS "cornball" country music show fashioned after the popular "Laugh-In" show on NBC.

Although Owens left the "Hee Haw" show to Roy Clark in 1986, he returned for their 20th anniversary show, and also retained his 400 episodes of "Buck Owens' Ranch." He was inducted into the Country Music Hall of Fame in 1996. His parent company still owns radio stations in Bakersfield, has two weekly publications, and the legend lives on at the Buck Owens' Crystal Palace.

Prior to his death March 25, 2006, Owens said he would be remembered "as a guy that came along and did his music, did his best and showed up on time, clean and ready to do the job, wrote a few songs, and had a hell of a time."

For information about Crystal Palace concerts, restaurant, museum, or Buck Owens' biography by Rich Kienzle, go to: www. buckowens.com.

Original 20 Mule Team Wagons
Originally built in Mojave, these wagons hauled Borax
out of Death Valley from 1883 to 1889.
During their years of operation,
these wagons carried over 10,000 tons of Borax
out of Death Valley, to Mojave.
Today, the U.S. Borax operation in Boron,
mines over 12,000 tons a day.

Sign at Borax museum

36

TWENTY MULE TEAM BORAX MUSEUM REINS US IN

Cruising down Highway 58 – east of Mojave in Boron, California – a sign we had seen dozens of times before, "Borax Visitor Center" drew us in.

The Borax Corporation – best known as the sponsor for TV show *Death Valley Days*, hosted by such notables as Robert Taylor, Dale Robertson and former actor, later president, Ronald Reagan. The museum devotes a display to the TV show, as well as providing product and ore displays, a short film, and a sample of borax – a piece of ore with interesting transparent properties.

For a token fee you can park inside the gate seven days per week from 9 to 5 – and take an hour to explore the past – when the twenty mule team wagons brought borax from Death Valley – or the present, where you view massive layered open-pits where massive trucks now haul out the borax.

Borax? Isn't that something our mothers used for laundry or cleaning?

Borax is an important compound of the element boron. Its chemical name is sodium borate or sodium tetra borate. It consists of soft, white, many-sided crystals that readily dissolve in water, and clump together when exposed to moist air.

Although Tibet is said to have been the first important source of borax, now, most of the world's supply comes from Death Valley and the open-pit mines in the nearby Mojave Desert.

In addition to washing powders, water softeners and soaps that contain borax – manufacturers mix borax with clay and other substances to make porcelain enamels for sinks, stoves, refrigerators and metal tiles. Potters use borax to add strength to their products and make a hard glaze for dishes and glassmakers mix it with sand so it will melt easily and provide strong, brilliant glass. We recently heard that mixing borax in equal parts with powdered sugar works as a deterrent for ants.

Borax may be taken from blasted, open-pit mines or from "dry" or "bitter" lakes where the brine, containing many salts, is pumped from the lake into containers. The heavy salts sink to the bottom, and the remaining brine crystallizes to refine borax. Solid borax taken from open-pit mines is crushed and dissolved, and goes through purification steps to obtain the crystals.

It is estimated that boron deposits formed 12 to 18 million years ago. The first boric acid was produced in 1702, and the element boron was isolated in 1808. F.M. "Borax" Smith discovered borates in Nevada in 1872 and in Death Valley in 1881. Twenty mule teams were established two years later to haul borax out of Death Valley.

An original twenty mule team wagon that the Borax Corporation used to haul ore out of California's Death Valley is on display outside the Borax Visitor Center. Pulling the wagon are twenty life-size, life-like mules – with a set of bells mounted on the lead mule.

Rio Tinto Borax operates California's larges open-pit mine in Boron. It is one of the richest borate deposits on the planet, supplying nearly half the world's demand for refined borates, minerals essential to life and modern living.

Next time you pass through Mojave or Boron, California, take a short trip off Highway 58 to visit the Borax Museum – and revive your interest in chemistry.

⚜

My country, 'tis of thee,
Sweet land of liberty,
Of thee I sing:
Land where my fathers died,
Land of the pilgrim's pride,
From every mountain-side
Let freedom ring.

"America" – Samuel Francis Smith

37

PRAY AS YOU GO

As we drove past a large white roadside sign with its black calligraphic words inviting travelers to "Pause Rest Worship," I commented, "Interesting!" The second time, we noticed a little white frame chapel with its steeple, set way back off Highway 95 heading south to Yuma in Arizona. Curiosity was getting the better of us. I said, "Next time we'll stop."

I question why it took us three passes before we stopped. Once we investigated we discovered that thousands of people already stopped and signed the guest books. Most of them probably passed that way but once. They heeded the call to pause, rest and worship. Maybe it was the worship part that prevented us from stopping the first or second time. The pause and rest parts were just fine. We do that all the time at highway "Rest Stops."

We were on a four-month motor home tour of the Southwest, escaping the harsh winter of Central Oregon. We spent a week at Martinez Lake, north of Yuma, and went in to town a couple of times. Leaving the lake the final time, I got my camera ready and we stopped at the little chapel in the middle of the farmland of Dome Valley.

Six polished wood pews and a modest pulpit made up the inside of the chapel. You go out the same door you come in. There are three windows on each side, and two green plaques with gold lettering on each side of a large plain wood cross behind the pulpit, and a guest book for visitors to sign. One of the plaques is "The Lord's Prayer" and the other is "A Farmer's Prayer," which tells the story of the chapel:

"Father, I thank you for the opportunity to serve you with this church house on the farm. I pray that you will use it to draw people to you. I pray that all believers in your Son, Jesus Christ, will feel free to worship you here together, and that this place might play a small part in bringing unity to your church. I thank you for the life you have given me filled with blessings from you. I especially thank you for my wife, Lois. She has been a true helpmate as we have farmed and raised a family together. I pray that many others will use this church to count the blessings you have given them. I humbly pray this prayer in the name of my precious savior, Jesus Christ."

The prayer and the chapel are dedicated to a farmer's wife of more than 40 years, mother of their three children and grandmother to six, Lois Pratt. Loren Pratt got the idea when he saw a roadside chapel while vacationing in the state of Washington with his family.

By April of '98, less than two years following the official opening of the chapel, one guest book had been completely filled by travelers from every part of the United States and visitors to the U.S. from other countries. At that time there were more than 2,000 signatures and messages. By April of the year 2000 that number can easily double.

It is so true, we pass this way but once. It is evidenced by countless guest books at resorts, historical sites and places of worship where we, as human beings, like to sign our names and leave evidence that we did indeed pass this way.

If you ever plan to motor west,
Travel my way, take the highway that is best.
Get your kicks on route sixty-six.
It winds from Chicago to LA,
More than two thousand miles all the way.
Get your kicks on route sixty-six.
Now you go through Saint Louie
Joplin, Missouri,
And Oklahoma City is mighty pretty.
You see Amarillo,
Gallup, New Mexico,
Flagstaff, Arizona.
Don't forget Wynona,
Kingman, Barstow, San Bernardino.

"Route 66" song make popular by Nat King Cole

38

FLAGSTAFF, ARIZONA – MORE THAN A ROUTE 66 LUNCH STOP

Flagstaff – a strange name for a city – refers to a Fourth of July celebration in 1876, when members of an exploration party stripped the branches from a tall ponderosa pine tree and displayed the American flag atop. The flag could be seen from a great distance and remained as a campground beacon for wagon trains headed to California.

Much later, a city grew up in the 7,000-foot elevation of the high desert foothills of the 12,643-foot San Francisco Peaks. Thomas F. McMillan was the first permanent resident, raising sheep after his arrival in 1876. Timber, sheep and cattle industry contributed to growth in the area until the Atlantic and Pacific Railway Company merged with the Southern Pacific line, reaching Flagstaff in 1882.

The impressive Tudor style railroad station that opened in 1926 now serves as a visitor center, where you pick up a walking tour map of the historic renovated late 1800 –early 1900 buildings in the surrounding old town district. Students from the Northern Arizona University may be seen with their books open on coffeehouse tables or while sitting on benches in the downtown park area.

Flagstaff, best known in relationship to "Route 66" song lyrics as being on the way to or from somewhere else, now encourages passers-through to stop and look around. Those history buffs who like to get their "Kicks on Route 66" will no doubt want to get stickers for their rigs and T-shirts when they stop in Flagstaff.

We were amazed at how much there is to see and do in Flagstaff. We took time in the late afternoon to stroll through the Old Town district, reading historic markers and picking out a restaurant from the menus posted on the windows and inhaling the aromas wafting out to the sidewalk. The next day we drove a mile up Mars Hill Road for a guided tour of the Lowell Observatory and a view of the city.

The observatory was founded in 1894 by Percival Lowell, whose observations about the planet Mars served as a basis for the theory of an expanding universe, and led to the discovery of the ninth planet, Pluto, in 1930. (Recently, Pluto was removed from the list of planets.) The guide told us Lowell spent most of his life at the site, and the 1923 observatory serves as his mausoleum.

The current, working observatory hosts a gigantic telescope mounted deep in a rotund amphitheater. We were allowed to look through the lens but not much is visible in daylight. Programs are offered for evening viewing.

We also visited the Museum of Northern Arizona and the Pioneer Museum – both located on N. Fort Valley Road, a short drive from the center of town. We enjoyed watching a group of school children exploring the exterior and interior exhibits at the Museum of Northern Arizona. Children, as well as adults, are fascinated with the prehistoric animal skeletons and rock formations. A highlight of the museum is the reproduction of a kiva – a meeting place and ceremonial room for Native Americans.

Across the street from the Museum of Northern Arizona we parked the RV and made a picnic lunch on the grounds of the Pioneer Museum, and then explored the grounds of a former hospital, built in 1908. Exhibits included farm machinery, medical equipment, toys and household items. Other buildings include a blacksmith shop, a cabin and a 1910 barn with a sheep wagon and a 1923 American LaFrance fire truck.

Flagstaff, nestled among pine trees and bordered by mountains, serves as a central location for day trips to Grand Canyon, Oak Creek Canyon (Sedona), Walnut Canyon National Monument or Wupatki National Monument. Those who still love the snow season from mid-December through mid-April may enjoy the nearby Flagstaff Nordic Center or the Arizona Snowbowl with its 2,300 feet of vertical drop, and an average snowfall of 260 inches.

Today's travelers can do as the pioneers did – stop where they see the American flag high on top of the pole, camp for the night and continue on to Nevada, California, Utah or New Mexico.

*The glories and the beauties of form, color, and sound
unite in the Grand Canyon –
forms unrivaled even by the mountains, colors that vie with sunsets,
and sounds that span the diapason from tempest to thinking ,
from cataract to bubbling fountain.*

John Wesley Powell

39

GRAND CANYON – LARGER THAN LIFE

It was nearly midnight, and the full moon lit up the sky for my first breathtaking view of Grand Canyon from Mather Point. The quartz in the white rock sparkled in the moonlight and I could see and hear people down below. I couldn't see all the way across the canyon, but I could see as far as Yaki Point.

Imagine how awe-struck the first visitors to the canyon must have felt. The first recorded viewing was in 1540 by a member of Francisco Vasquez de Coronado's expedition. While searching for the Seven Golden Cities of Cibola they chanced upon the massive gorge.

It was late May of 1869 when Major John Wesley Powell led the first expedition to explore the length of the canyon. He and his nine boatmen left Green River, Wyoming, on the Colorado River and six of them emerged into open country at the western end of the canyon August 30.

The persistent flow of the Colorado River over the past six to 25 million years has carved the Kaibab Plateau in northern Arizona to an average depth of one mile. The force of the river has exposed cliffs, vistas and canyon walls of incredible color and beauty.

Grand Canyon is 277 miles long, averages 10 miles in width from rim to rim, and is 5,700 feet deep on the North Rim, which averages 1,200 feet higher than the South Rim. It might better be called "canyons" because of its massiveness, endless views and photo opportunities. You can see it from an airplane, a helicopter, or a river raft on the Colorado deep inside the walls of the canyon. You can hike as far as you want and return the same day, or you can backpack or ride a mule to the canyon floor and camp or stay overnight at the Phantom Ranch.

Visitors have been known to walk up to the edge at some point on the North or South Rims, look down into the canyon, return to their cars and boast, "Okay, now I can say I've seen Grand Canyon." It is not a destination; it is an experience – more than a one-stop photo opportunity.

I once had a co-worker who backpacked deep into the canyon every two to three years. It was where her spirit had found a home. Oh to be young again, and explore the heights and the depths of this amazing place. Most of us content ourselves with the more limited – but no less awesome – experiences from the edge.

Each year nearly five million people visit Grand Canyon – mostly from overlooks along the South Rim, including Grand Canyon Village, Hermits Rest Road, and Desert View Drive.

The South Rim, 60 miles north of Williams and 80 miles northwest of Flagstaff, Arizona, is open all year. Backpacking hikers who go deep into the canyon on selected trails can cross the Colorado River at a narrow foot bridge to get to the North Rim. Unless you can fly, the only other way from the South Rim to the North Rim is to drive the 215 miles around the East Rim Drive. Well worth the trip, with its many scenic stops. It takes about five hours, not including stops for viewing.

The morning after the full moon experience we, my daughter Carol, granddaughter Angela and I, hiked about three miles down the Bright Angel Trail – took pictures, ate our sack lunches, watched other hikers as well as the birds and small animals. Then I huffed and puffed my way back up the trail. Younger legs and knees might have gone deeper into the canyon. People riding mules on the trail looked like they were having a much better time of it. Next trip I'll hop on board and leave the driving to wagonmaster on the mule train.

There are signs at the rim telling, or warning people about the distance and importance of carrying plenty of water. The temperature rises as you go down into the canyon.

Grand Canyon is divided into three basic areas – the South Rim, the North Rim and the Inner Canyon. Average elevation at the South Rim is 7,000' above sea level. During June, July and August the temperature on the South Rim is in the 80s. Then the temperature begins dropping by 10 degrees each month thereafter. Most campgrounds, the Grand Canyon National Park Visitors Center and IMAX Theater, lodging and other facilities are open all year. Reservations for National Park Service-operated campgrounds should be made five to six months in advance by phoning DESTINET at 800-365-2267.

In August the Inner Canyon can be over 100 degrees in the daytime and drop to the 70s at night. By October the Inner Canyon cools to the low 80s in the daytime and the 50s at night. Anyone planning to backpack anywhere in the park, or camp below the canyon rim, must obtain a permit from the Backcountry Office.

The North Rim is an entirely different story, because of the higher elevation, on average over 8,000' above sea level, it is much cooler and wetter than the South Rim. The North Rim is open and accessible mid-May through mid-October. It remains open for day use only through December 1, or until heavy snows close the road. There will be no food, gasoline or lodging available at the North Rim after mid-October.

Free shuttle buses at the South Rim make life easier. Minibus service along West Rim Drive and around Grand Canyon Village is available from Memorial Day through September. Passenger vehicles are not permitted along West Rim Drive during the summer months. Sight-seeing tours are available for a price from hotels and other locations. For more information, go to www.grandcanyon.com.

After our little Bright Angel hike we were more than ready for a minibus ride out the West Rim Drive to Hermits Rest where we watched the sun set and cast pink, purple and orange shadows and highlights on the canyon walls. We took the minibus from the visitors Center and were returned to the parking lot.

The next day we took the East Rim Drive all the way to Jacob Lake. There were many stops at outlooks along the way. We paused at Yaki Point, Grandview Point, Moran Point and the Tusayan Museum & Ruin. I started down the road to the North Rim, through forests of white- limbed Aspen with leaves turning yellow in September. I knew we couldn't make it all the way to the North Rim and back before dark so we only went half way. After dinner at Jacob Lake we arrived after dark in Mt. Carmel, Utah, and the following morning we began out next adventure through Zion National Park.

Whether you view Grand Canyon from the top, the bottom, or along the Colorado River – at sunrise or sunset, or during a full moon light show – it is called "Grand" for a reason. You must see it to believe it and, to have the true canyon experience.

Once more I am roaring drunk with the lust of life
and adventure, and unbearable beauty…
Adventure seems to beset me on all quarters
without my even searching for it…
though not all my days are as wild as this,
each one holds its surprises,
and I have seen almost more beauty than I can bear.

Everett Ruess, early Glen Canyon explorer

40

GLEN CANYON DAM/LAKE POWELL – SOMETHING FOR EVERYONE

Driving more than 100 miles north from Flagstaff on Arizona Highway 89 you will cross the Colorado River on the Glen Canyon Dam Bridge at Page, and soon reach the south-central Utah border heading for Zion National Park and Bryce Canyon – but, do stop and enjoy the spectacular Glen Canyon National Recreation Area and Lake Powell.

From its very beginning, the construction of the Glen Canyon Dam aimed at meeting the hydroelectric needs of a diverse population of American communities, industry and private citizens.

Before the first blast occurred at the dam site on October 15, 1956, the area was virtually inaccessible, and construction crews were forced to drive 200 miles to cross from one side of the canyon to the other. The Bureau of Reclamation engineers and geologists worked for two years in selecting the site that would contain an immense amount of water, with canyon walls strong enough to support one of the world's highest dams.

By 1959, trucks began crossing the Glen Canyon Bridge to deliver equipment and materials for the dam and to the new town of Page, Arizona. Placement of buckets of concrete continued day and night for three years. Each bucket held 24 tons of damp concrete, and it took over 400,000 of those buckets to fill the dam. According to historians there was enough concrete poured for the dam and power plant to build a four-lane highway from Phoenix to Chicago.

It took three years to install the turbines and the dam was dedicated by Ladybird Johnson on September 22, 1966. It took 17 additional years for the creation of one of the world's largest man-made lakes – Lake Powell – to completely fill for the first time.

The Carl B. Hayden Visitor Center rotunda is located at one end of the Glen Canyon Bridge and visitors may tour the historic project free of charge. An elevator takes you 528 feet deep into the interior or the dam. At one point on the tour there is a digital counter registering the money collected from the sale of power throughout the region. The plant generates more than 1.3 million kilowatts of electricity with each of the 40-ton steel shafts turning at 150 rpm, generating nearly 200,000 horsepower. There are eight generators.

To fully enjoy all the recreational benefits provided by the formation of Lake Powell, touring the Hayden National Park Service Visitor Center will add an appreciation of the magnitude of this $272 million project. Glen Canyon Dam not only controls the upper Colorado River flow and generates electricity for countless households and businesses, but also has repaid the United States Treasury, with interest.

Our approach to Lake Powell was from Page, Arizona, on the east side of the canyon. We entered the Glen Canyon National Recreation Area through the South Wahweap fee station and had a full hook-up at the Wahweap Campground. Wahweap has 90 full hook-ups and 112 tent or non hook-ups. To check out additional camping or boating options go to www.nps.gov/glca.

According to the brochure from the new Lake Powell Resorts & Marina:

"Lake Powell nourishes all your senses – from the feeling of pristine fine-grained, salmon-colored sand between your toes, to the sight of a night sky twinkling with infinite stars and planets.

With nearly 2,000 miles of shoreline, over 90 major canyons to explore, and the world's most famous natural stone bridge – Rainbow Bridge National Monument – Lake Powell is America's Favorite house boating destination. A memorable place to fish, hike, camp, paddle, sightsee, photograph, powerboat, water-ski, and, of course, relax and reconnect with family, friends and Mother Nature herself."

Houseboats and powerboats are a preferred way to enjoy Lake Powell with its many niches, and are advertised as easy to operate. A variety of scenic cruise adventures can take 1-1/2 hours on the Antelope Canyon or 7-1/2 hours on the Rainbow Bridge Cruise. Depending on the lake water level passengers may see the Bridge from the water or walk in 1-1/2 mile. Cruises depart from the Wahweap Marina. For information and reservations go to www. lakepowell.com.

We were at Lake Powell in the spring, on our way to Bryce Canyon. Rock formations and colors on the shores of Lake Powell were a striking prelude for the awesome experience of Utah's other amazing canyons and landscapes.

The true test of civilization is,
not the census,
nor the size of cities,
nor the crops,
but the kind of man that that country turns out.

Ralph Waldo Emerson

41

GOING BACK ONE THOUSAND YEARS – CHACO CANYON, NEW MEXICO

RVers and campers have the opportunity to experience the ancient Puebloan culture that flourished a thousand years ago in northwest New Mexico by staying in a campground inside Chaco Culture National Historical Park.

At Canyon Overlook Trail above Gallo Campground, you can watch the brilliant desert sunset. Stay until dark and you may hear the distant drumming of the Pueblo ghosts. In the morning, birds welcome the new day as the sun shines on Fajada Butte Solstice Marker, Chaco Canyon's dominant landmark, revered by the Pueblo people, and off-limits to visitors.

Gallo Campground sits amid a high desert landscape surrounded by petroglyphs, a cliff dwelling and inscriptions inside Chaco Culture National Historical Park, which preserves one of America's most significant areas.

Chaco Canyon was a major center of trade and ceremonial life of the ancestral Puebloan culture between 850 and 1250. The inhabitants constructed massive stone buildings, called "great houses" that contained hundreds of rooms and multiple stories. Dozens of houses in the canyon were connected by road to 150 great houses built in outlying areas.

More than 400 miles of prehistoric roadway have been identified. The roads required engineering and planning and represented a significant investment in construction and maintenance. One of the longest segments of road heads north to the communities of Salmon and Aztec.

Isolated Location

To reach Chaco Culture National Historical Park, you must travel over unpaved roads. The National Park Service says it is leaving the roads unpaved to keep park visitation at a manageable level, protect cultural resources from deterioration, devote park funds to ranger tours, hikes and talks, and maintain a casual and relaxed atmosphere.

According to the National Park Services, "We believe that traveling 15 or 22 miles on a dirt road is a small price to pay for the kind of park experience that is fast disappearing from our American scene."

The recommended route to the park is from the north, via U.S. Highway 550 and County Roads 7900 and 7950. The trip includes 16 miles of rough dirt road.

Be sure to have a spare tire and a good road service policy. Our flat tire occurred on Highway 550 after leaving the rough roads of Chaco Canyon behind. We received fast service out of Farmington. If you don't want to take your RV into the canyon, there are several RV parks in Farmington.

The Tour Begins

As you travel from Nageezi in the north on dirt and gravel roads, you come to a nine-mile long paved loop drive that provides access to Chacoan sites. Your first stop after getting an information brochure at the National Park Service gate should be at the Visitor Center museum.

After viewing a film, you will drive along the one-way paved interior road to the trailheads for the following sites: Una Vida, Hungo Pavi, Chetro Keti, Pueblo Bonito, Kin Kietso, Pueblo Alto Complex, Casa Chiquita, Penasco Blanco, Pueblo del Arroyo and Casa Rinconada Community.

Pueblo Bonito is a featured attraction whether you have a few hours or an entire day. By the year 500, the nomadic Anasazi began the pueblo at the base of the northern canyon wall, and by the 10th century it was four stories high with more than 600 rooms and numerous kivas (ceremonial or council rooms generally below ground level). Casa Rinconada, one of the largest kivas in the Southwest, is located in the central area of the canyon and may have served communal needs.

Pueblo Bonito—Spanish for Beautiful Town—united many diverse peoples serving as the cultural, spiritual and trading center for the Hopi, Navajo, and other Puebloan people from present-day New Mexico, Colorado, Utah and Arizona. Pueblo Bonito typifies the Chacoans' great architecture and masonry.

Researchers estimate the year-round population for the pueblo at 50 to 100—and around 2,000 to 6,000 for the Chaco Canyon as a whole. They base their estimates on the number of habitation rooms with fire pits, and the quantity of pottery vessels.

Evidence of Skilled Builders

Today's travelers owe a debt of gratitude for the architectural and masonry skills of the Native Americans who built and maintained the great houses, kivas and roadways in and around the Chaco Canyon.

Working with stone tools, they erected vast communal buildings. The earliest dwellings were built with simple walls one stone thick, held together with generous courses of mud mortar. When they began to build higher and more extensively, they employed walls with thick inner cores of rubble and thin veneers of facing stone.

The walls tapered as they raised, evidence of their construction planning.

Chaco's distinctive Cibola black-on-white pottery may have originated in outlying towns to the south and west and been brought to Pueblo Bonito for trading. Turquoise was used by craftsmen for beads, necklaces, pendants, and some pottery.

Though they moved from the canyon in AD 1100, probably due to drought, they are not forgotten—and many Southwest Indian peoples consider Chaco a sacred place where clans gathered for friendship, trade and spiritual connection.

For information about the park, road conditions and Gallo Campground, visit www.nps.gov/chcu. The campground has 48 dry-camp sites, of which 15 are tent-only. The sites are available on a first-come-first-served basis. Sites cannot accommodate trailers or motor homes more than 30 feet in length, as there are no pull-throughs. There are two restrooms with flush toilets, but no showers. Non-potable water is available at the camp. Drinking water is available in the Visitor Center parking area. Two group campsites for 10 to 30 people each can be reserved.

Question. What dost thou chiefly learn by these Commandments?
Answer. I learn two things: my duty towards God and my duty
to my neighbor.
My duty towards my Neighbour, is to love him as myself,
and to do to all men, as I would they should do unto me.

Church of England Prayer Book – 1662

42

BUILDING IN BAJA, AND OTHER LIFESTYLE CHANAGE

Growing up in the Midwest, if anyone had asked me the location of Baja California, I might have told them it was part of the United States' lower West Coast. When I moved to California in the 1950s I found out otherwise.

Never, in my wildest dreams did I think I'd be spending winters on that Mexican peninsula.

In 1998, my future husband Harry Taylor and I closed up our Oregon houses to travel the Southwestern states in his Roadtrek RV. We were exploring possible future winter locations. While in Yuma, Arizona we picked up a flyer at the tourist center. For $99 we joined an escorted caravan in El Centro, California, traveling to San Felipe, Baja California Norte, included was a week's stay at the El Dorado Beach Club Resort and RV Park, along the Sea of Cortez.

We had planned to skip Mexico, but bit the bullet and bought Mexican auto insurance. That changed our lives.

We weren't immediately hooked by the sales pitch and tour of El Dorado Ranch. But, after spending the next week on the beach in town we went back to the ranch and bought, or rather acquired, a 20-year-renewable lease on a lot in a solar energy community. At the very least we were getting a membership in Coast to Coast Resorts of America with RV parking, and a potential investment.

During our two week stay we were captivated by spectacular sunrises on the Sea of Cortez, dark star-filled nights, and tides going out a quarter of a mile for clamming. We ate good food and met friendly people. A plan to build on the lot came later.

Throughout the remainder of our trip through Arizona, Nevada and California we talked about our lot in Mexico. By the time we reached our summer home in Oregon, we had roughed out a plan for a 600 square foot stucco cinder block house. We faxed the drawing to the contractor at El Dorado Ranch. He, in a month's time, sent us his preliminary plan, a punch list and pricing. We made changes and later signed the contract and a check for work to start.

By the time we reached the ranch that year we were pleased to see the shell of a house with a roof. Then we waited and waited, and waited. Everything was done on Mexican time. Meanwhile we lived in the RV Park at the ranch and participated in the good life – playing tennis, swimming in the pool, clamming, hot tubing and visiting Juanita's Cantina for music, food and fun. We moved in four weeks before it was time to head north again.

The following year we had a house to go to, and had fun furnishing with put-it-together-yourself and second-hand pieces.

A lot of Mexican brick was laid down for patios front and back, as well as bordering our washing machine tub fire pit.

We stand at our front door and see the Sea of Cortez a mile away. From our roof deck we have a 360 degree view of the sun rising out of the sea, the sun setting behind Montana Diablo, and on the darkest of nights we see constellations and shooting stars.

In San Felipe we attend monthly meetings of the San Felipe Association of Retired Persons (SFARP). No relation to AARP. At one meetings Olivia, a Mexican architect and high school principal, spoke to us about building houses in the area.

Olivia assists Americans and Canadians who have come to San seeking a lifestyle change in what once was a poor laid-back fishing village.

Many of the "Gringos" are full-time RV travelers following the sun for a place to park for the winter. Although they have escaped from a permanent address north of the border, they are finding it more difficult each year to book into spaces after the first of the year. Most travelers reserve space in Arizona, California, and other southwestern states several months or a year in advance.

So, how does Olivia the architect help these transplants from the north? Although she isn't the only show in town, she has counseled and worked with a significant number of potential and current homeowners in San Felipe.

"People come to us looking for comfort," Olivia speaks very good English but still struggles with some of the words. "The mistake people make is trying to build a house like they would in their own country.

"We start with their needs. How much space will you need inside your house?" she asks, pointing out that living space doesn't necessarily include a large garage. "The husband may want a garage for his tools and toys. The wife may want a larger kitchen or bathroom." Olivia acts as a mediator. "An architect is like a psychologist. Stopping the disagreement between the husband and wife while building," she said.

Negotiating space allocations for furniture and determining how you will move around for comfortable living is part of the equation. The cost and best use of materials is another.

"Most Americans and Canadians are accustomed to building with wood," said Olivia. "Wood is expensive. We want materials that help get the heat in when it's cold outside and keep the heat out when it's hot outside." Houses are primarily constructed of Mexican brick, cinder block, other new materials, or straw bale. People are outside as much or more than inside their houses.

In San Felipe we are 124 miles to the border, and travel by RV to El Centro, California or Yuma, Arizona once a month for a few days. We shop at the military base, Costco or Wal-Mart, go to a movie and have dinner. And use our cell phone to call family. And, because we are based so close to the border we can take the RV out and travel to the Mexican mainland or to California, Arizona, Texas or New Mexico.

Since this was written early in our Mexican experience, we now drive a car and stay at motels along the way. The cost of gas and lodging mostly evens out. Generally, we spend one week in Palm Springs on our way down and take care of medical contacts. As we age, we consider how long we intend to travel to a second home in Mexico. We love it, but we are realistic.

The fine and noble way to destroy a foe,
is not to kill him;
with kindness you may so change him
that he shall cease to be so; then he's slain.

Aleyn – English poet (1590-1640

43

THE ART OF SWATTING THE FLY IN SAN FELIPE

The first rule of fly swatting in San Felipe is not to assume anything. The fly is pesky, persistent and powerful. And, for the sake of this instruction I refer to the fly in the generic "he" or "him." Just as I refer to God as He, because I really don't know for sure one way or the other.

Rule 1

Do not assume that just because there is a fly, or many, in your sphere of influence that you MUST swat the creature. You may wish to contemplate the order of creation and the food chain. Are you denying some other creature food, or is there an abundance of flies? Also, by not engaging in the swatting game you may outwit him. If we humans are intelligent beings, maybe we can psyche-out or wait-out the annoyance of a fly on the end of the nose or perched on the edge of the coffee cup.

Setting all that philosophical stuff aside, you have determined to engage in warfare. The fly, every last fly, must die.

Rules 2 through 5

2. Purchase a good fly swatter, one with a sturdy handle that doesn't bend when on the attack. Make certain the swatting surface is not curled or bent, as this may impede the process. Such instruments of fly destruction come in many designer colors. You may wish to purchase them in quantity so that other members of your family can engage in the sport, or so that you may have these instruments in several rooms of your home. Always ready to swat.

3. If for some reason you are not up for the real sport of fly swatting, you may wish to purchase fly strips. Those ugly, sticky things, that hang from light fixtures and doorways. And, I might add, those sticky things that catch in you hair (should you be fortunate enough to have hair) when you aren't looking, or ducking.

Or, if you have a really mean streak in you, you may spray the entire house with some noxious chemical. Again, fly swatting at least gives the creature a fair warning and half a chance for escape to the great outdoors. Now, if you were a fly, wouldn't you rather be outside instead of continually bumping up against a window or screen in a futile attempt to leave, since he obviously made a mistake entering in the first place.

4. Now, let me give you some real techniques. Do not assume that just because you have swatted a fly once, and he is writhing in pain on the floor, don't assume he is done. I have seen many a fly get up and go when I thought he was down for the count. He may require a second swatting to give him a proper send off and put him out of his misery.

5. Watch the fly carefully before you strike. Eventually, he will land on a surface where you have a good shot at him. The rim of a cup or somewhere on your own person or the person of your spouse will not do. We all have reflexes that make it nearly impossible to hit ourselves and get away with it.

Hopefully, you will corner the fly on the counter top or cupboard door. A swift swat and he falls or is pushed into the sink, and down the drain. Or, better yet, hit him where he will drop to the floor. Then you can sweep him away with a broom or gently scoop him up in a tissue and give him the Royal Flush.

A reminder, fly swatting can be addictive. I actually made a decision not to pick up a fly swatter for 24 hours. My husband didn't think that was sporting and kept his fly swatter handy. So, for me, it became a spectator sport for that one day. Another reminder, fly swatting can consume you and can result in obsessive and compulsive behavior. You will become paranoid, seeing flies where there are none. In fact, I have a "floater" in my right eye that sometimes takes on the appearance of a fly rather than half a spider web.

Also, if you are building a house in San Felipe, and you have workers coming in and going out on a regular basis, the flies are the least of your concerns. Relax a little. Enjoy the sunlight and the fresh air. If all the flies are in your house, why not go outside.

Oh, as an afterthought don't forget to take your snake stick.

O Captain! My Captain! Our fearful trip is done,
The ship has weather'd every rack, the prize we sought is won,
The port is near, the bells I hear, the people all exulting.

O Captain! My Captain! – Walt Whitman

44

THE TITANIC SINKS
AGAIN IN BAJA, MEXICO

Just before midnight on April 14, 1912, the White Star liner Titanic, on its maiden voyage from Southampton to New York, struck an iceberg and sank, leaving 1,513 dead.

Then, came the 1997 blockbuster epic film *The Titanic* with romantic leads Leonardo Dicaprio and Kate Winslet, and the disappearance of the fabulous deep blue jewel pendent – the only thing Winslet was wearing when sketched by Dicaprio.

Fox Studios Baja, located on the edge of the Pacific Ocean along the Rosarito-Ensenada Scenic Road about 45 minutes from San Diego, was originally built for James Cameron's award-winning movie about the sinking of the Titanic, its passengers and survivors. Foxploration adjoins the studio and offers the public an inside/behind-the-scenes experience of filmmaking at this self-contained production facility with some of the world's largest stages and filming tanks.

Although the huge replica of the Titanic was built and subsequently sunk for the movie, the studio preserved or reproduced entire rooms – and of course the necklace – to allow visitors an inside view.

Fox Studios Baja continues to play host to moviemakers, and because movies are in production there are some off-limits areas. In addition to *The Titanic*, scenes from the following films were shot at Fox Studios Baja: *007-Tomorrow Never Dies* (1997, MGM); *In Dreams* (1997, Dreamworks); *Deep Blue Sea* (1999); *Weight of Water* (2000, Phoenix Pictures, with Sean Penn & Elizabeth Hurley); *Pearl Harbor* (2001, with Ben Affleck); and *Masters and Commanders* (2003, with Russell Crowe.

Through the magic of smoke, mirrors, electronics and push buttons, members of our tour group prevented a couple of miniature ships from a colliding under a fog bank in a large tank of water. Viewing the action on a monitor made it look like it was taking place in the ocean. We also participated on the sound stage with thunder, creaking doors, gunshots and galloping horses.

Hollywood doesn't have the last word on tourist attractions. Foxploration invites you to explore the world of movie magic as you "pass through our gates and enter a new world where imagination and reality merge."

You can stroll down Canal Street, New York – a real movie set street. There you can enjoy Domino's Pizza, a Subway sandwich or Tepoznieves Ice Cream.

Cinemagico is the interactive journey through movie making. Dolly Plaza has the original fountain from *Hello Dolly*. Fox/JVC presents behind-the-scene footage of recent Fox films. See what actors use on sets in the Props and Wardrobe Bodega.

On weekends, the studio's Las Olas Open Air Amphitheatre offers performances by local musicians and artists, with the Pacific Ocean for a backdrop.

A short trip down Mexico way offers an enjoyable experience for adults and children of all ages. Foxploration's regular hours are Wednesday, Thursday and Friday, from 9:00 a.m. to 5:30 p.m; Saturday and Sunday, from 10:00 a.m. to 6:30 p.m. For additional information, check: www.foxploration.com.

They are not long, the weeping and the laughter,
Love and desire and hate:
I think they have no portion in us after
We pass the gate.
They are not long, the days of wine and roses:
Out of a misty dream
Our path emerges for a while, then closes
Within a dream.

Ernest Dowson (1867-1900)

45

ON THE RUTA DEL VINO, GUADALUPE VALLEY

Tecate, the beer that made the northern Baja city of Tecate famous, comes from the Cauhtemoc Brewery on the outskirts of town, 32 miles southeast of San Diego. This oldest and largest brewery in Mexico was established near the Tecate River in 1943 by Mexican businessman Alberto Aldrete, and now shares its fame with up-and-coming-winemakers from the Guadalupe Valley vineyards.

The Ruta del Vina, or route of the wine begins south of Tecate and stretches through scenic countryside bordered by low rolling hills on Highway 3. Thousands of Mexican, American and Canadian wine-tasters visit the Baja Wine Country annually.

A *Baja Times* map cites 17 major wineries along the Ruta de Vino. Our tour included the two largest wineries, and two unique wineries. Plenty of vino for one day.

Although 80 percent of the two million plus cases of Baja wines per year are consumed in Mexico – Baja Wine Country Tours with San Diego Wine and Culinary Center are increasing the awareness of these world class wines by bringing motor coach tours into the Guadalupe Valley.

According to *Baja Times,* "Wines from Mexico are imported in bulk and mixed with San Diego County wines creating unique international hybrid wines. Grape vines from Escondido, California were planted years ago in Baja and wine consultants from both countries are currently trading knowledge, equipment and technology.

Settlers originally came to the area because of the abundant water and fertile soil. Farmers and ranchers created a center primarily for growing olives, grapes and grains. Later, Tecate became an industrial area for making beer and processing of coffee.

During the 1917 prohibition of the manufacture, sale or consumption of beer, wine or whisky in the United States until its repeal in 1933, Mexican border towns saw an increase of activity, revenue and growth thanks to visits from their U.S. neighbors

Casa Pedro Domecq Winery

In 1972, Pedro Domecq, the producer of El Presidente Brandy, founded the first modern commercial winery at the northern end of the Guadalupe Valley. His plan to produce inexpensive wines under a variety of labels resulted in the Padre Kino, Los Reyes, Calafia and the X-A lines. More recently, the Casa Pedro Domecq Winery has begun to improve and expand its Reservada and X-A lines of premium wines.

Three categories – Premium, Fine, and Lower Alcohol Content – are produced by the Casa Pedro Domecq Winery. According to the winery "the objective of the lower alcohol content wines is to achieve wines with full aromas and color, with a style resembling French Beaujolais. They must be very fresh and lively, with a light body and easy to drink, wines that can be included in any occasion."

L.A. Cetto Winery

In 1926, two years after engineer Angelo Cetto arrived in Tijuana from his native Italy, he founded a wine-bottling business. In 1945 his eldest son Luis Ferruccio Cetto began exporting fortified and table wines by trucking cases of wine from Tijuana to Ensenada where they were loaded on ships southbound to Acapulco on the mainland. Cases of wine were then trucked to Mexico City over rough roads.

The Cetto family acquired the first 250 acres in the Guadalupe Valley in 1960, followed by the purchase of a 180-acre vineyard that was planted in 1930 with Zinfandel cuttings from southern California. The L.A. Cetto holdings have since grown to over 2,500 acres in the region under the operation of Angelo's son Don Luis Augostin Cetto.

On a trip to Italy in the early 1970s Don Luis hired a young Italian winemaker named Camillo Magoni, who was trained in northern Italy's Piedmont region, followed by the study of clonal varieties of the Nebbiolo grape at Nino Negri in northern Lombardy. Magoni's first task was the selection of acreage for planting classic varieties such as Cabernet Sauvignon, Merlot, Petite Sirah, and among the whites: Chardonnay, Sauvignon Blanc and Chenin Blanc.

Don Luis and Magoni agreed that the Guadalupe Valley's Mediterranean climate was conducive to the cultivation of Italian varieties. The first bottles of wine bearing the name "L.A. Cetto" appeared in 1983, nearly a decade after the first plantings. The further introduction of red wines occurred in 1993 with the debut of their Syrah, Sangiovese, Petite Verdot and Malbec, as well as the new white Viognier wine.

Cetto is Mexico's largest producer of table wines with sales of over 840,000 cases annually and distribution to more than 29 countries, as well as a display of more than 75 award winning medals since 1992.

Dona Lupe Winery AKA Rancho La Gotita

The Dona Lupe Winery, down the road from L.A. Cetto, offers visitors a rare opportunity to purchase herbs, pies, jams, salsa, and freshly baked cookies in her wine tasting room and gift shop. She planted the vineyard herself over 30 years ago and practices organic and biodynamic farming. She boasts that the purest water in the region combined with rich riverbed soil produces high quality organic grapes.

Dona Lupe's son Daniel Yi creates unique and interesting wines. He leaves the grapes longer on the vines to benefit from the extra natural sugars in the grapes. Try Dona Lupe's Cabernet Sauvignon, Zinfandel, Grenache, Merlot, as well as the Port wine.

Vinos Bibayoff Winery

Walking on the grounds at Vinos Bibayoff makes this out-of-the-way winery worth the drive over rough roads. Members of the Russian Molokan community arrived in the Valley around 1906. They were mainly wheat growers. Subsequent immigrants planted vineyards for the production of table grapes and wine. In the 1930s Alexie M. Dalgoff obtained a permit to make wine. By the early 1970s his grandson David founded Vinos Bibayoff winery.

Although most of their Red Globe table grapes are sold off to other wineries, David Bibayoff will pour generous samples of their five estate wines that have spent some time after fermentation in French oak barrels. Weather permitting he places several bottles and glasses on top of an empty barrel or two and serves you among the trees.

Secure a Guadalupe Valley map of vineyards to guide your palate to additional wineries. Roads are well marked with names and directions to vineyards, and restaurants.

The City of Tecate

Tecate's recorded history began in 1831 when a Peruvian named Juan Bandini obtained a land concession of 18 square miles from the Government of California, when all of California belonged to Mexico. With a population of more than 60,000 Tecate is unlike other border towns, having retained much of the "Old Mexico" charm while adding fine restaurants and hotels. Gigantic boulders jut out of the hillsides throughout the city, and many of the structures, such as the outstanding Plaza Santa Monica Restaurant in the Polimeros Formula, are built around and incorporate rock formations.

Tecate's border crossing is relatively painless compared with Tijuana or Mexicali. Your shopping time and money will be well spent at Rancho San Pablo – shops include Chavez Pottery, Montiel's Clay, San Pablo Clay Products and Tecate Ceramic. It's hard to resist taking home something you've watched being made.

And, if you are so inclined, be sure to visit the ultra-modern Cuauhtemoc Brewery– where the beer that made Tecate famous is brewed.

How to get to Ruta del Vino

- From Tecate travel 43 miles south on Route #3 to Ruta del Vino.
- From San Diego/Tijuana take toll road #1 south through three toll booths toward Ensenada. Before entering Ensenada take Route #3 about 18 miles toward Tecate.
- Tecate border crossing – Check the hours for US and Mexican customs.
- Cuauhtemoc Brewery tours are given on Saturday mornings.
- Tecate is home to world famous spa Rancho La Puerta and Rancho Tecate Resort.
- Tecate has a KOA campground.
- In May, thousands of cyclists from both sides of the border participate in the annual Tecate-to-Ensenada bicycle race.
- In July there is a two-week celebration in Los Encinos Park, Tecate.
- Further information: www.baja-web.com/tecate, www.ranchopuerta.com, Wine Tours email: sbdryden@hotmail.com, www.bajatimes.com.
- If you take your vehicle into Mexico you must have Mexican auto insurance. Check on current U.S. passport requirements for returning to the U.S. Ask your travel agent about tours to Tecate and the Guadalupe Valley Wine Country.

Roll on, thou deep and dark blue Ocean – roll!
Ten thousand fleets sweep over thee in vain;
Man marks the earth with ruin –
His control stops with the shore.

Lord Byron (1788-1824)

46

ROCKY POINT – ARIZONA'S CLOSEST BEACH RESORT

Puerto Penasco, Sonora, Mexico – better known as Rocky Point to Americans vacationing on the eastern coast of the Sea of Cortez (Gulf of California) since the 1920s – is a mere 60 miles from the Arizona border crossing town of Lukeville.

Arizona RVers and vacationsers looking for relief from the summer heat frequently head south to Mexican sea coast towns rather than west to the Pacific Ocean or north to the woods and lakes. The web site www.rockypointonline.com touts the headline "Arizona's Closest Beach Resort…and best kept Secret" to offer potential visitors information about food, lodging, weather and points of interest.

For additional local information and local color you can go to the *Rocky Point Times* newspaper at www.rptimes.com.

Of the several RV parks listed in the *Trailer Life Directory* we stayed at Playa de Ora and Playa Bonita, both with beach frontage where we could see the sun set. From the RV Park at Playa Bonita it was a short waterfront walk to their hotel and the Puesta de Sol Restaurant. There, we enjoyed a wonderful shrimp dinner while watching the sun set and listening to music of happy hour entertainment.

Long before Americans discovered Rocky Point; retired Lt. Robert William Hale Hard of the British Royal Fleet sailed along the coasts of Sonora and Baja California (Mexico) in 1826, searching for pearls and precious metals. On marine maps, he identified the area as Rocky Point. Later, Mexico's future president General Lazaro Cardenas changed the name to Puerto Punta Penasco (Port Rocky Point). Americans dropped the Port and Mexicans dropped the Punta.

Built in 1927, Rocky Point's Posada La Roca Hotel in the historic Old Port section of town claims to have been the hiding place for Al Capone during prohibition in the United States when he was seeking a port of entry for his bootleg liquor. Still a working hotel, the attendant showed us a comfortable room with its thick, soundproof rock and mortar walls.

During the early 1920s Americans traveled from Tucson, Phoenix, Gila Bend and Ajo to catch the enormous flying fish. Commercial fishermen traveled up the coast from Guaymas, Mexico to El Golfo de Santa Clara at the mouth of the Colorado River north of Rocky Point to find protection from storms and a beautiful and tranquil estuary. Once potable water was available they began fishing the waters around Rocky Point.

Prohibition in the United States gave rise to bars, clubs, hotels and casinos where thirsty Americans were welcomed to the border towns. Capitalizing on the craze, John Stone, who owned a hotel in Ajo, Arizona, decided to build a hotel-casino in the Rocky Point area. He had a well dug and sold potable water to the fishermen and local residents. He built an airport and established Scenic Airlines. The town was born and later died when Stone had a falling out with the fishermen and left them high and dry – burning down the hotel and blowing up the well.

In 1936, President Cardenas visited the area, took pity on the poverty-stricken residents, and made plans for a wharf for cargo vessels, a railroad to unify it with the Baja and the rest of the country, and a highway to the United States. The well and the old Stone Hotel were revived, urban development began, and luxurious hotels, shops and restaurants grew up.

Although Arizona would have preferred keeping this shrimping village for its very own sea port and resort area the Mexican government kept it during negotiations following the 1846-48 territorial wars between Mexico and the United States. The Mexican President Antonio Lopez de Santa Anna did not want to give up territory that would separate mainland Mexico from the Baja California Peninsula.

Over the past 25 years, Puerto Penasco has become increasingly Americanized, with thousands of visitors coming south and becoming property owners. Playa Las Conchas hosts an enormous development of American owned white "mansions" on the white sandy beaches overlooking the Sea of Cortez.

There are people on the Malacon and Old Port streets offering free dinners, reduced-price dinner cruises, or gas certificates to get tourists out to the Mayan Resorts – Mayan Palace and Grand Mayan. Resort property and condominium sales have become big business in Rocky Point.

Other sights or places of interest are Lupita's Candy Store, Santana's Coffee Shop, Curios Wendy (if you can't find it there it doesn't exist), the small aquarium, Pinacate Desert National Park biosphere reserve and the 30-year-old Desert and Ocean Studies Center (CEDO).

The University of Arizona is the primary research and educational user of CEDO, together with the University of Texas at El Paso, two community colleges and Biosphere II. CEDO's in-house program monitors weather conditions, the distribution and abundance of intertidal organisms, beached marine mammals, as well as alternative fishing activities to minimize threats to endangered species.

Information about CEDO, their programs, tours and hours for the Earthship Visitors Center contact www.cedointercultural.org. CEDO's role is to study, teach and protect the ecosystems of the Upper Gulf of California and Colorado River Delta Biosphere Reserve. With human progress sometimes come threats to the environment.

According to CEDO's statement, "Reduced freshwater, declining nutrient flow and diminished water quality along with poorly-managed, non-selective fishing practices are the greatest perils to this once-rich ecosystem." There is a concerted effort by both Mexican and American business interests, biologists and ecologists to develop Rocky Point and at the same time protect the ecosystem that attracts so many visitors to this resort area.

Puerto Penasco's beaches, sometimes rocky, stretch for miles. Although summer temperatures are hot, the clear, warm coastal waters invite visitors from California, Arizona and New Mexico to shop and dine, as well as sail, snorkel, parasail, and scuba dive and swim year-round.

One man scorned and covered with scars
still strove with his last ounce of courage
to reach the unreachable stars;
and the world was better for this.

"Don Quixote" – Miguel de Cervantes

47

GUANAJUATO HOSTS ANNUAL INTERNATIONAL CERVANTES FESTIVAL

The next time we go to Guanajuato, in Old Colonial Mexico, I hope to be there during the Cervantes Festival, Latin America's most important annual cultural event.

Each year, for more than two weeks in October, the city welcomes visitors from around the world who come to participate in or enjoy a vast array of performing and visual arts – symphony, ballet, opera, live theater, as well as presentations of art, literature and photography.

In 1972, the first Cervantes Festival was devoted primarily to artistic creation in the Spanish language, and named to honor Miguel de Cervantes, Spanish author of *Don Quixote*. Cervantes' novel is considered a first in modern literature, and has been translated into numerous languages and adapted to live theater, movies and musicals.

The city also hosts the impressive Don Quixote Iconographic Museum, as well as the Instituto Miguel de Cervantes. The institute provides intensive language study and practical-immersion experience for individuals and groups. Upon request, you can learn about Mexican history, literature, art, and even Mexican cooking and Latin dances.

Cervantes Festival performances take place in each of the city's three main theaters, and at the University of Guanajuato. Construction of the majestic Teatro Juarez – its neoclassical façade crowned with bronze statues of Greek muses – began in 1872 and was completed in 1903. Events also take place at Teatro Principal and Teatro Cervantes, as well as several of the city's beautiful churches, in its plazas, or in the streets themselves.

The University of Guanajuato originally was founded by the Jesuits in 1732 as the College of the Holy Trinity, and became the property of the Government of the State of Guanajuato in 1828. Many prominent Americans have attended the University of Guanajuato, a centerpiece for the city's cultural activities. Florida Governor Jeb Bush met his wife while attending Guanajuato University and the tour guide mentions several other well-known persons, along with President Jimmy Carter's daughter Amy.

We visited this city of unparalleled beauty and history as part of our bus tour to Old Colonial Mexico, where the revolutions against both France and Spain were fostered.

Our 21-day mid-winter tour with 30 of our San Felipe neighbors on a brand new Mexican bus was put together by Americans living in Mexico for more than 20 years.

Traveling into the heartland of the Mexican revolutions opened my eyes to the marvelous history, culture and architecture of the country that has the U.S. as neighbors to the north and an entire continent of Latino culture to its south. Although we visited Alamos, Guadalajara, Dolores Hidalgo, Leon, San Miguel de Allende and Matzalan, we are partial to Guanajuato.

Guanajuato was home to the Otomi and nomadic Chuchimecas tribe until the Fifteenth Century when the Spaniards discovered the rich silver mines. The city takes its name from the Purapecha language – Guanajuato means "hilly city of the frogs."

In 1548, Juan Rayas changed the destiny of the area with his discovery of silver. In 1741, the city was given the title of "The Most

Noble and Loyal City of Santa Fe y Real de Mines de Guanajuato" and became the country's richest area in the Sixteenth Century because of its gold and silver mines. In 1988, UNESCO designated Guanajuato "A World Heritage Zone."

A city tour with an English speaking guide took us to the Valenciana mine, with its 525 meter shaft still in operation, and which at one time produced more than two thirds of the silver mined in the city.

Our hotel, the Howard Johnson Parador San Javier, is located on the lavish hillside grounds of a former hacienda belonging to a silver-mining company owner. On Sunday morning we took a short walk up the hilly street behind our hotel to the Santa Cecilia Castle, now an impressive hotel with a fine restaurant where we had brunch.

Guanajuato overview from high above the city.

One of our morning excursions took us bouncing over a winding rough road in an uncomfortable small tour bus to the Cristo Rey, Christ the King Monument – at the highest point in the Bajio Valley, atop the Cubilete Mountain. It is said to be located at the center of all Mexico. Construction on the Bronze sculpture – 66 feet high, weighing 250 metric tons – began in 1923. Cristo Rey stretches out his arms from atop the church dome towering over the plaza, with a panoramic view of. Mexicans on pilgrimage walk on their knees across the tile plaza into the Salve Regina Church.

Another day, another 12-seater tour bus took us to the Mummy Museum, where 119 mummified bodies are encased in glass. The first body was exhumed in 1863. They were preserved as a consequence of the peculiar mineral composition of the region's soil. This is a unique but spooky place and our visit was short.

Guanajuato is a network of 17 former mine tunnels that were cut through mountains and later converted to streets to relieve the flow of automobile traffic. In addition there are underground streets winding along a dry riverbed. The Guanajuato River flows through a tunnel deep beneath the city streets, alleys and buildings.

City residents take pride showing off their many picturesque walk-through alleys – whether you go by day or on a lighted night tour with strolling, student minstrels. And, you'll need directions to find The Kiss Alley, where two balconies nearly meet.

We visited beautiful churches with their wooden altars, still aglitter with gold. We drove through posh neighborhoods occupied by Americans, Canadians and Europeans, and ended our tour at the Pipila (torchbearer) Monument, above the center of town. The gigantic statue of Pipila honors Juan Jose de los Reyes Martinez, a hero of the Mexican independence who on September 28, 1810 set fire to the door of the massive granary that the Spaniards used as a garrison.

While we were high above the city the guide took our picture for our annual greeting cards. Then we rode the Funicular down to the Jardine de la Union. This town square was filled with restaurants and visitors and it was alive with roving, energetic mariachi bands. We had lunch at Van Gogh's Ear. A walk around town led us to the Diego Rivera, Don Quixote Iconographic, and People's Art museums.

It was late February, the week before Easter, and the people were celebrating, but then, there are festivals all the time in Guanajuato.

How to get there and what to do

Guanajuato is located twenty-five minutes from Leon International Airport (BJX). There are international flights to Leon from the United States via Dallas, Houston, Los Angeles, Oakland, and Chicago. Other options include flights to Mexico City or Guadalajara, with connecting flights to Leon. To explore best fares try www.exitotravel.com. A bus from Mexico City takes about four hours. Guanajuato is in the Central Time Zone.

Other web sites may include entering the following: Guanajuato, Instituto Miguel de Cervantes, or Cervantes Festival.

While in Mexico, tourists should always carry documentation regarding their citizenship. All tourists traveling 25 miles into Mexico must obtain a tourist visa (FM-T). Students planning to stay more than 180 days should go to the nearest Mexican consulate well in advance of their travel.

Clothing for Guanajuato is relaxed, comfortable, and requires a good pair of walking shoes. The city is more than 6,000 feet above sea level. Some people require a day or two to adjust to the altitude. As expected, exercise caution regarding drinking water and fruits and vegetables that you can't peal or purify.

Generally, you get more bang for your buck if you use pesos, credit cards where possible, and ATM machines to get pesos. As with all travel to foreign countries, be aware of your surroundings and personal safety.

Australia is properly speaking an island,
but it is so much larger
than every other island on the face of the globe,
that it is classed as a continent
in order to convey to the mind a just idea of its magnitude.

Charles Stuart

48

TAKE YOUR TIME IN AUSTRALIA AND NEW ZEALAND

You say you always wanted to go to Australia and New Zealand. Well, what are you waiting for? When it's autumn in North America it's springtime "down under." Or, vice-versa, if you like skiing in Queenstown, New Zealand. And, you'll be satisfied with the exchange rate.

Since getting there is such a huge expense, take your time, because Australia is a huge country. We most often find we haven't allowed enough time to take advantage of being there, wherever "there" happens to be. We discovered no advantage to round-trip air, train or bus travel in country or between countries, as one-way airfares are reasonable.

If you book an all-inclusive, one-price-fits-all, package of flight, ground transportation, meals and miscellaneous entertainment fees and expenses you will know in advance you will be in Sydney for four days, have a bed to sleep in and a hot meal at six every evening. Then off you fly to somewhere in New Zealand for another chance to be herded about on planes and buses. Some people need, want and can afford that kind of predictability and security. We like the challenge of making it up as we go along and interacting with people who live and work in countries we visit. Everywhere we went in Australia and New Zealand we met friendly and helpful people

If you are an able-bodied backpacker, Australia and New Zealand will love you, welcome and accommodate you. They will even help you find short-term employment and hostels. If you are retired senior citizens like us, with the luxury of time, you may be able to travel for less.

For our trip "down under" we parked our motor home at Travis Air Force Base near Sacramento, California, on November 1, and fortunately, caught a military Space-A flight out the next day. (A benefit for retired military.) Space-A means you go when and where they make room for passengers. With a 28-hour layover at Hickam AFB, Hawaii, three-hour layover at Pago Pago (pronounced Pongo Pongo), American Samoa, and the loss of a full day because of crossing the International Dateline, we arrived in Richmond, Australia, on November 4.

The next morning we took a train from Richmond to Sydney. Train fare is cheaper after the morning commute hours. We planned to stay in Sydney at least seven days. When we arrived at the Central Railway Station we each bought the seven-day "Triple Pass" for unlimited travel by suburban train, bus or ferry boat. We used a credit card at every opportunity. The statement came a month later and we were pleased with the bank's exchange rate.

At the train station in Sydney we were directed to a large reader board with hotel, motel, and hostel listings. I picked up the phone there and called Central Railway Motel. Steve answered and said I had called the best hotel in Sydney and, once we stayed there we would never want to leave. His friendly manner and good directions brought us by cab to his doorstep. We hit pay dirt with our room, bath, kitchenette and TV. We were in the Strawberry Hills renovated district that hosts bistros, coffee shops, curbside eateries, and an Internet Cafe.

The next morning we realized we were conveniently located walking distance from the train station. We travel light. Our small backpacks have handles and wheels, so we pulled them along when needed. Since our triple passes were good day and night in and around Sydney we didn't need a car. Thus, avoiding problems with traffic and parking.

We frequently took the train from Central to Circular Quay Station. From there we walked or took one of the numerous ferry boat rides in and out of the harbors. As the sun set, the sky turned golden, then at dark, background for the harbor and city lights.

We saw three great Australian movies, went to the symphony at the world famous opera house, visited the animals at the Tonga Zoo and explored museums. From a second floor window of The Rocks historical museum you can see the Governors Mansion through a space between buildings across the Sydney harbor. Here, Governor Arthur Philip established the British penal colony of New South Wales in 1788. The Rocks became a lawless and disease-ridden area. Today it hosts artists, specialty shops and fine restaurants.

We took a full-day bus tour to the Blue Mountains, with stops at the site of the 2000 Summer Olympics, a wildlife zoo where we had our picture taken with a sleepy Koala Bear, and a sheep station to watch the round-up, practice boom-a-rang throwing, and drink Billy Tea.

After a week in Sydney we were faced with choices. We knew we lacked time for the Outback, or Melbourne, so we opted for a trip to Brisbane, a city of many culinary surprises along its winding river. Round-trip airfare, three nights at a great hotel across from Albert and Wickham Parks and a short walk to the Queen Street Mall, plus four-day car rental cost less than $250 each. We drove up the Sunshine Coast to Noosa Heads one day and down the Gold Coast to Tweed Heads the next. Miles of white sandy beaches, covered with young bodies during Schoolie Week (or Spring Break) in Australia. We limited our time on the beach as we were told the sun is very intense "down under."

While in Sydney we booked a very reasonable flight and camper van rental package for New Zealand. We flew Air New Zealand into Christchurch. The Pacific Horizon Travelhomes people picked us up at the airport and we spent an hour going over the contract and details of the vehicle. Don't expect the kind of luxury you have with motor homes in the USA. These are compact and efficient touring vehicles. Ours was small. You either sit at the table or make up the bed. We picked up our maps, got our bearings in kilometers, and were on our merry way – driver on the right and hugging the road on the left.

While touring in the United States we seek out natural hot springs. In New Zealand, we headed straight away to the Hanmer Springs, north and west of Christchurch. Many New Zealanders, or Kiwis, take their holidays at Hanmer, a place not likely to be part of a tour package. We had a glorious soak in several of the outdoor pools that night. The following morning I viewed a spectacular sunrise across the meadow and over the mountains. We stayed in the first of the many Holiday Parks we were to call temporary homes. The RV parks are independently owned and operated but required to meet the same standards.

Touring the South Island offered an up-close and personal view of the natural beauty the country offers. Campervans and backpackers were everywhere. You can park a van overnight at any beautiful scenic area on public land. There are great distances between RV parks. Although our little van had shower and toilet, we preferred a shower where you weren't bumping your elbows on the walls or your shins on the commode.

After Hanmer we headed west to Greymouth then south along the Tasman Sea. We stopped at the artisans' and jade shops in Hokitika. Parkas were more appropriate than shorts as we passed by Franz Joseph and Fox glaciers and icy running streams. The coastal road ended at Haast, where we turned back inland toward Queenstown, the summer and winter sports Mecca of the South Island. It's a bustling town with so many wonderful restaurants. We had lunch at the Hard Rock Café. We were parked overnight near the tram to the ski slopes and there was a dusting of snow on the surrounding hilltops in the morning.

Friends who have been to Australia and New Zealand have told us they loved New Zealand. We agree. The camper van is the best way to see the countryside. Hillsides and valleys were covered with golden spring wildflowers that looked like Scotch Broom but didn't smell like it. Lupine in shades of purple, pink, yellow and white blanketed the roadsides and meadows. Lupine grows tall and thick, and sheep dot every green landscape. Because it was spring "Down Under" little baby lambs were tagging along with their mothers in all the meadows. We stopped frequently just to drink in the overwhelming freshness and beauty of nature.

We went back to Christchurch for a day and a half of walking and driving about the city, attending a service at Christ Church, and making the last call for latte at Starbucks on a Sunday afternoon. We didn't have enough time to go everywhere and see everything. It takes more than a week to see the best that New Zealand has to offer. We never toured the North Island, nor did we get to the Fiordland National Park or Milford Sound. But then, that gives us a reason to go back someday.

After an overwhelming and almost unanimous vote by Gibraltarians
to reject plans by London and Madrid to share sovereignty over the Rock,
BBC Monitoring looks at what is being said in the media
in both Gibraltar and Spain.

BBC Online – 8 November 2002

49

TERRITORIAL DISPUTE OVER "THE ROCK" OF GIBRALTAR

When Americans think of "The Rock" they think of the Prudential Insurance Company. When the British refer to "The Rock" they are talking about Gibraltar. When the Spanish hear someone refer to "The Rock" they become angry, they want that piece of Spain back.

But, the British say, "Never!"

"The Rock" of Gibraltar wasn't even on our list of places to see during our five weeks touring Europe by automobile in 2003. It wasn't even mentioned in our AAA tour book. But then, we probably would have looked under Spain, because it occupies two-and-a-half square miles of the southern tip of that country, jutting out into the sea.

The British, however, acquired "a piece of The Rock," or as a matter of fact, all of "The Rock," in 1704 when they captured it during the War of the Spanish Succession. Britain confirmed its hold on Gibraltar in 1713 by the Treaty of Utrecht, and it still is a British Crown Colony, and home to their important naval base.

During the American Revolution, when both France and Spain were at war with Britain, "The Rock" withstood a three-year siege.

When I think Gibraltar, I think Prudential Insurance – and I guess in advertising terms that means something permanent and solid. And, I had some clue that it was a strategic location during World War II, thus an attraction for veterans. During the Nineteenth Century its value as an invulnerable naval base, with extensive tunnels to the Mediterranean, was strengthened, and it hosted an air base as well during World War II.

The straits separating Gibraltar from Africa are only fourteen-and-a-half miles wide, and whoever controls "The Rock" controls the gateway between the Mediterranean Sea and the Atlantic Ocean.

"The Rock's" limestone cliffs rise more than 2,400 feet above the sea, but their height was not a deterrent for the Muslim leader who crossed from Africa in the year 711 to begin the conquest of Spain. "The Rock" was named Gibraltar, a corruption of Djeb el Tariq (the hill of Tariq) in honor of that Muslim leader, and remained in the hands of his followers until its Fifteenth Century conquest by the Spanish.

Had we planned ahead we would have spent more time in Gibraltar, because its history and physical location are fascinating. We are the pick-up-and-go kind of travelers and sometimes miss great places, great photo opportunities, and reasonable hotel rates. We've had to accept the fact that we can't do it all or see it all.

It was evident by the lines of traffic trying to park at Gibraltar on the morning of September 11, 2003 that a lot of people planned ahead and knew where they were going, and what they expected to see and do. Later, we saw all the British flags and streamers hanging from the buildings, noting that on the previous day Gibraltar celebrated its "National Day." And, if Spain dreams of ever getting "The Rock" back, the British continually say "never."

We parked on the street with parking meters rather than snake in a line of cars about two miles around the bay. We were there less than a day and had to hustle. Following are a few handy hints we wish we had known in advance:

- Have your passport handy. You cannot get into Gibraltar without it. An airstrip runs across the main road into the city just past customs, and gates may close for 15 to 30 minutes to hold pedestrians back while a small plane lands or takes off.

- Plan ahead for lodging, and for some of the tours such as the lower St. Michael's Cave; the World War II Tunnels used by Gen. Eisenhower to invade North Africa; as well as Dolphin Tours. The nearest Spanish city is Algeciras.
- Travel across the straits to Tangier, Morocco is sometimes on the "not recommended or do not travel" list put out by the U.S. State Department.
- Britain is not on the Euro. Other currency will go through the current exchange rate. Credit cards are best where accepted.
- If you go early, you can try to find parking at one of the lots or on some of the streets. If you choose not to drive, you can take a bus, taxis or minibus to get oriented. It's a long walk, even if it is only two-and-a-half square miles.

Tourist attractions in this little colony

Rock Tours; The Convent, official residence of the governors since 1728; The Great Siege Tunnels, impressive defense system for evacuation; World War II Tunnels used by Gen. Eisenhower; Shrine of Our Lady of Europe and Museum, originally a mosque; The Museum, with 200 million years of history; Parson's Lodge, ammunitions depot; Europa Point and light house; St. Michael's Cave, natural grotto; The Marinas; Moorish Castle; The Gibraltar Botanic Gardens; Trafalgar Cemetery; City Center; Dolphin Tours; and The Rock Apes, home to famous Barbary Macaques.

Only in Europe can you go through Spain to get to the British Colony of Gibraltar, be a stone's throw away from the African continent, and get such a huge slice of history. It's worth taking your time.

The pact of Munich was a more fell blow to humanity than
the atom bomb at Hiroshima.
Suffocation of human freedom among a once free people,
however quietly and peacefully accomplished,
is more far-reaching in its implication and its effects on their future
than the destruction of their homes, industrial centers
and transportation facilities.
Out of rubble heaps, willing hands can rebuild a better city;
but out of freedom lost can stem only
generations of hate and bitter struggle and brutal oppression.

Dwight D. Eisenhower

50

PRAGUE – "GOLDEN CITY" SURVIVES NAZISM AND COMMUNISM

Entering the Czech Republic on our way to Prague (Praha) from Austria, we were required to show our passports at a check point for the first and only time while touring Europe for five weeks by automobile.

Prague Castle background for Charles Bridge musicians.

None of the old fears of Communism have existed since what is now referred to as the "velvet revolution" grew on the streets of Prague from a whisper to a roar heard around the world on November 17, 1989. University students and sympathizers were commemorating the 50th anniversary of the closure of Czech universities by the Nazis when the officially sanctioned event broke up and 5,000 participants decided to march to Wenceslas Square in New Town. Communist riot police tried to break up the crowd. There were injuries but no deaths. Hundreds of thousands Czechs rallied for a week of demonstrations, until the Communist regime crumbled.

Vaclav Havel, poet, playwright, political dissident and first post-Communist president wrote for an August 2003 *Time Magazine* special issue on Europe that "this day was not a bolt out of a clear sky." …. "No one knows which inconspicuous snowball has the capacity to set off an avalanche, which, to the surprise of all observers, will radically change the political situation."

Most visitors to the newly opened borders of Eastern Europe head for the major cities in Poland, Romania and Czechoslovakia (Czech and Slovak republics since 1993). Understandably, because history is waiting to be discovered. Travel agents put together beautiful packages to see these cities by plane, boat and train. Train travel in Europe has long been a preferred choice for Americans in Europe. This time, we chose the auto.

We rented a small car at a reasonable rate out of Ramstein Air Force Base in Germany. Everyone drives small cars. Gas mileage is good. They perform well on expressways, on narrow city streets, and are easy to park. Left lanes are for passing only on expressways, and you have to get out of the way for fast moving cars. Most rest stops are full service with food, gas and even hotels. Rental agencies have rules about what cars can go into which countries. For instance, Mercedes cars may not be able to go into some Eastern European countries.

Prague, formerly referred to as Bohemia, has played host to Good King Wenceslas, the Hussite Wars, the Habsburg rule, Hitler's Nazi Party in 1938, the Red Army "liberators" in 1945, and 40 years of suppression by the Communist Party from 1948 until the

"Velvet Revolution." Fortunately, 1,000 years of medieval building facades, castles, bridges, Gothic spires, cobbled passageways and alleys survived occupation and earned colorful Prague the title of "Golden city.

Most European cities have rest stop/information centers where we sometimes made hotel reservations. However, it took about 90 minutes, in the rain, to find our hotel in Prague. The street maps were hard to follow because we found the language difficult. It's best to ask directions from young people, more likely to have been exposed to English in school.

The Czech Republic suffers from a shortage of hotels and hostels. Many of the Communist-era hotels are being overhauled. Reservations are recommended during the International Music Festival in May and early June, and when the Orthodox churches celebrate Easter. Signs saying "Zimmer Frei" indicate bed and breakfast in a private home. We found in Europe it was best to drive to the City Center, park, and start looking for lodging.

Continental breakfast is nearly always included in the price of your hotel room. We generally eat a hearty breakfast, substantial late lunch, and something light for dinner. Most Europeans do it that way. Wonderful international cuisine choices abound in Prague.

Finally arriving at the Alfa Hotel, we parked the car and took public transportation or walked from there during our stay in Prague. The hotel clerks spoke good English and provided helpful information. We enjoyed a fine dinner a few blocks away in a basement restaurant we never would have found on our own. The hotel clerk booked our city tour for the following morning. A minivan took us to the center of town and we boarded a tour bus with an absolutely delightful 80-year-young Czech woman who "fills in as needed, as I need the money." Gratuities are gratefully accepted everywhere, especially in Eastern Europe.

The Czech Republic, a member of the European Union, had not yet converted to the Euro dollar. Meanwhile their currency, the Euro, US dollars, and credit cards worked.

The Prague Castle complex and St. Vitus Cathedral deserve a whole day of touring, as do the Old Town Square with the white

Church of St. Nicholas and the Astronomical Clock on the Old Town Hall. On the hour a skeleton appears and chimes the bell, followed by the 12 Apostles and other characters. Leaving the Square in search of the famous Charles Bridge, we lost ourselves on Karlova Street. Window shopping and checking on restaurant menus was part of that experience.

More than just a river crossing, on Karluv (Charles Bridge) you will see 30 sculptures, puppeteers, souvenir sellers, The Bridge Band, and an organ grinder with a monkey puppet. The 1,700-foot span was built in 1357 and provides a spectacular view of the river and of the city's domes and spires.

Four distinct towns grace both sides of the river. They joined together in 1784 to form central Prague, and there are 15 bridges crossing the Vltava River.

In Prague you can visit *Metamorphosis* author Franz Kafka's diminutive house on Golden Lane; bask in the grandeur of Chram svtecho Mikulase (St. Nicholas' Church) where Mozart played the 2,500-pipe organ in 1787; shop for puppets or Bohemian crystal, porcelain, lacework and ceramics; or simply appreciate the city and tradition that produced such composers as Antonin Dvorak.

The Czech Republic is known as more than a country of diverse landscapes locked between Poland, Germany, Slovak Republic and Austria. It boasts of such charming medieval towns a Ceske Budejovice (home of Budweiser beer). And, Prague – the Golden City, in 2000 designated a European City of Culture – and home to a proud and patient people who overthrew 40 years rule by the Communist Party – a warm and friendly population eager to be discovered by travelers.

Twenty years from now you will be more disappointed by the things you didn't do than by the ones you did do. So throw off the bowlines, sail away from the safe harbor. Catch the trade winds in your sails. Explore. Dream. Discover.

Mark Twain

AFTERWORD

Snowbirds Unlimited: Tales from the Restless Traveler merely scratches the surface of a lifetime of travel at home and abroad, coupled with ten years of documenting portions of that travel in columns and articles.

Deciding where to begin and end, and what to put in the middle of a book is a daunting task. Readers may think it comes together well enough, or wonder at its somewhat random selections. Most books begin somewhere way back in the memory, until the nagging will not let the writer rest until a commitment is made to pursue the project. If readers look for a theme, that theme is me, these are my observations of the world in which I find myself, and the world I love to explore.

The assembly of material began when I spread out all the folders of published articles and columns on the pool table which shares my office space in the outbuilding we never quite know what to name. Some sense of organization that exists only in my own head guided me over the many weeks of sorting and entering manuscripts from mostly already existing copy on my computer.

Of the four books I have self-published to date, this probably was the easiest from a purely mechanical perspective. Since a majority of the material already existed, I simply (or not so simply) searched, highlighted, cut, pasted, reviewed, edited and put it in the lineup. I'm always amazed when something comes together.

Many interesting, exotic and wonderful destinations are missing from this book due to the space limitations, or they just didn't make the cut because I would have to write an entire new piece to include that particular adventure.

In April of 1996, I went on a pilgrimage to Israel with a group of Episcopalians from Portland, Oregon. We prepared for nine months through reading, lectures and learning music that required no accompaniment. I have audio tapes and photos, and memories beyond expectations from that trip. Two months prior to that trip I had back surgery, and then my mother died less than two weeks before we left for The Holy Land, Jordan, and Petra.

My trip to London in 1997 was a cultural and educational experience. My friend Norma and I stayed at the Penn Club, near the London University and the area where Virginia Wolfe and other famous intellects lived. I heard the Nightingale sing in Barclay Square, visited the Tower of London, the London Museum, and saw the "Buddy Holly" musical. I flew out of London for Glasgow, Scotland, rented a car and traveled to the Highlands and the Isle of South Uist where my father's ancestors left in the early 1800s.

Harry and I have been to Tokyo, Japan twice and from there to Singapore once. The air pollution in Tokyo depressed us and the cleanliness of Singapore dramatically impressed us.

We traveled extensively in Europe. In 2003 we mostly drove from one country to another. On that journey we were so taken with Prague that we wanted to see more of the Eastern Block countries that once were in the grips of Communism. So, in 2006 we booked a tour of those countries bordering the Danube River from Budapest, Hungary to Bucharest, Romania. We learned how fortunate we in America are to have been spared that kind of domination and devastation.

We have covered much of mainland Colonial Mexico, as well as Cancun on the Yucatan Peninsula. Mexico's ancient pyramids and temples are awesome.

And, because we hadn't seen enough pyramids and temples, we took a ten-day tour of Egypt in April of 2010. The heat and the pace of that tour sometimes left me breathless. Though Egypt was on the top of my bucket list, and I didn't want to miss a single event, I had to stay on the bus at least once. It is a trip requiring strong legs and constitutions – a bit younger perhaps. Our first morning on the Nile River I woke early, went to the top deck and surveyed the landscape with a gentle breeze on my face, I said to myself "This is why I am here."

Although the days of family-travel slide shows in the living room have passed, we now have social networking to share our enthusiastic reports and photos online. And, if some of us are fortunate enough to do what I am doing, and readers are interested enough to buy the books – we still can share in the adventure.

Made in the USA
San Bernardino, CA
29 October 2014